KT-545-060

FLORAL KEEPSAKES

Preserving
&
Arranging
Dried Flowers

FLORAL KEEPSAKES

PRESERVING & ARRANGING DRIED FLOWERS

by

Sunny O'Neil

SEDGEWOOD® PRESS   NEW YORK

For Sedgewood® Press:

Director: *Elizabeth P. Rice*
Project Manager: *Barbara Machtiger*
Project Editor: *Sydne Matus*
Production Manager: *Bill Rose*
Cover & Book Design: *Jos. Trautwein/The BookMakers Studio*
Photography: *Mark Gulezian*
Line Drawings: *Cynthia Petrowski*

Copyright ©1990 Erma Wilkinson. All rights reserved.
Distributed by Meredith Corporation, Des Moines, Iowa.

ISBN: 0-696-02331-8

Library of Congress Catalog Card Number: 89-061408

Printed in the United States of America

10   9   8   7   6   5   4   3   2

DEDICATION

This book is dedicated to
SYLVIA STINSON,
without whose friendship and flowers
it could never have been written.

ACKNOWLEDGMENTS

My heartfelt thanks go to Ralph, my loving husband, and my sister Delora, who gave me help and inspiration.

I am grateful to my many friends who came to the rescue with advice and flowers. I want them to know how important they are to me: Don Haynie, Tom Hamlin, Frances Boone, Helen Wiseman, Larry Davis, Quentin Steitz, Madeleine Siegler, Bobbe Pearson, Harriet Flotte, Ralph Cramer, Ida Mae Chadwick, and that computer whiz Don Essick.

Dear Crafter:

We are so pleased you have chosen *Floral Keepsakes,* and we are sure you will be too. The spectacular dried flower arrangements inside are surprisingly simple to make. All the information you need is laid out for you—from the how-tos of drying to the flower-by-flower instructions for arranging.

There are beautiful floral displays for all occasions—table centerpieces, wreaths, holiday and gift arrangements large and small, wedding flowers, and special effects that include such unusual items as topiaries and adorable floral bears.

Sedgewood Press produces craft books of the highest quality. We offer a range of projects that will appeal to crafters of every skill level—from beginner to expert. All books feature color photographs, extremely clear instructions, and a variety of designs and uses. We are very proud of *Floral Keepsakes* and hope you'll experience many enjoyable hours poring over it and using it to create your own lovely dried flower arrangements.

Sincerely,

Barbara S. Machtiger
Editorial Project Manager

CONTENTS

INTRODUCTION

*D*ried flowers add much to our store of winter decorations at a time of year when fresh flowers are expensive. They have a special place at parties because dried flower centerpieces and decorations can be made weeks before the event, allowing the hostess to concentrate on the menu and other details, and are lasting mementos once the occasion has passed.

The idea of dried flowers as colorless, dusty things is old hat. Just by glancing through this book you can see boldly colored designs and sweetly delicate ones. Almost any form can be created with dried flowers—wreath, wedding bouquet, basket trimmed with or filled with flowers—the list is endless.

First things first, we begin by explaining the techniques of flower drying and describing the various tools and materials you will use most often, many of which you already have around the house.

You will learn how to create gorgeous displays to complement any space, spectacular centerpieces and table arrangements, quick-and-easy wreaths, complete wedding flowers, decorations to beautify holidays year round, gifts for every occasion, and out-of-the-ordinary shapes and designs.

Even if you don't raise your own flowers, or are a gardener with a brown thumb, you can buy fresh flowers or pick wild ones, dry them, and turn them into long-lasting floral masterpieces. The flower-by-flower instructions will help you experience the exhilaration of seeing your creation "grow" before your eyes.

The process of flower drying is a form of magic: Burying a fresh flower in sand and unearthing it a week later dried is exciting. You have many happy hours of working with dried flowers ahead of you. I envy you the thrill of just beginning.

—S.O'N.

THE BASICS OF PRESERVING AND ARRANGING

Here's everything you need to begin creating your own dried flower arrangements—techniques, materials, and encouraging words.

DRYING AND PRESERVING FLOWERS

Dried flower arrangements should be planned in the spring when the first flowers start to blossom, then created in the fall with the fruits of your harvest around you to serve as inspiration. Welcome and preserve each wave of bloom from gardens, meadows, roadsides, and farm markets. Pick and dry a few flowers every day, rather than set aside a flower drying day when it will surely rain or someone will have to go to the dentist. Spend the summer adding to your collection of dried flowers and leaves, always drying more than you think you'll need. Dried flower arrangements require two or three times as much material as fresh bouquets. And some flowers are always lost in the drying process. The projects in this book list the number of dried flowers needed; to be safe, dry twice as many.

Try to pick flowers to be dried at their peak of bloom or just before. Select the most perfect flowers you can find; flowers that are damaged or beyond their prime will not dry well. Flowers must be thoroughly dry when picked. Cut flowers after the dew has dried, but before the heat of the sun makes them droop.

If your garden is not large, plant the standard, easy-to-grow flowers that always dry successfully, such as marigolds, zinnias, and nigella. To guarantee some color in the garden, plant a few flowers that do not dry well. Good choices are forsythia, azaleas, petunias, cosmos, gladioli, and chrysanthemums, as well as succulents like portulaca and bearded iris. Ask a friend to grow her favorites so you can trade, either before or after the flowers have been dried.

Many markets have inexpensive fresh flowers for sale that you can dry to enhance your arrangements. Just be sure the flowers are fresh. Be on the lookout for farms featuring pick-your-own flowers along with the fruit and vegetables. Many wild flowers and grasses dry well, with goldenrod at the top of the list. Goldenrod, by the way, has gained a bad reputation among people with allergies, but ragweed is actually the culprit. They often grow side by side. The lightweight ragweed pollen floats unseen through the air while the highly visible goldenrod gets the blame. Goldenrod pollen is heavy and falls harmlessly to the ground.

Because they take up so much growing space, it is more feasible to purchase dried baby's breath, German statice, and other commercially dried "fillers" now on the market.

Working with dried flowers is ideal for the novice arranger, since the flowers won't wilt or die. The bouquet can be stopped and started again a week later. If the finished arrangement isn't quite up to the arranger's standards it can be taken apart and put back together again. If a stem breaks, another stem or wire can be added to it. If everything goes wrong the flowers can be broken up for potpourri.

Once you start drying flowers, the sheer enjoyment of it will take over, and along with it the tendency to pick and dry everything in sight. You'll find that in addition to adding bursts of color to your own winter days, you'll be making dried bouquets to give away as gifts and as donations to bazaars. So let the habit overtake you—and enjoy yourself.

The three most often used mediums for drying flowers are air, sand, and silica gel. Most flowers and grasses can be air-dried; sand is used for drying flowers whose original shapes must be preserved; and silica gel is for drying the more delicate blossoms, such as lilies of the valley, roses, and peonies.

Some arrangers opt to use other mediums to dry their flowers. But after years of experimenting, I have found that they caused various problems:

Borax clings to the flowers and must be laboriously removed with a dry paint brush; Kitty Litter is too coarse and pits the petals; and cornmeal slightly wrinkles flowers dried in it. So, I have personally settled on sand and silica gel as the two most successful drying mediums.

Whatever method of drying is used, some color changes will occur. As a rule, reds turn at least two shades darker and pinks with a blue cast turn lavender. Most other colors remain true.

The photographs on pages 11 and 12 show flowers that were dried in the air; pages 13 and 15 in sand and in silica gel.

Air-Drying Flowers

Drying flowers in the air is the oldest, most commonly used, and easiest method of preserving them. Most of the flowers and grasses used in the beautiful dried flower arrangements seen in shops, craft shows, and garden catalogues are air-dried. Flowers dried by this method are the backbone of

Air-dried flowers. From top row to bottom, left to right. *Row one:* craspedia globosa, strawflowers, peonies, yellow everlasting; *row two:* lavender, scabiosa, red salvia, poppy seed pods; *row three:* chive blossoms, nigella pods, pink globe amaranth, orange globe amaranth; *row four:* curry plant, carthamus tinctoris, astilbe, blackberry lily.

designs that feature specimen flowers, such as roses, zinnias, and marigolds, which are dried in sand or silica gel.

The most suitable place for drying flowers is in a warm, dry, dimly lit room, like an attic. Heat does not seem to harm the flowers but humidity causes them to mildew during the drying process and to fade and grow limp after they are dried. A dehumidifier will help keep moisture out of the room and away from the flowers. Bright sunlight should not be allowed in the drying room because it fades the flowers, both during and after the drying process.

Flowers to be dried should be free of moisture, and have their leaves (which become brittle and slow down drying time) removed. Pick the flowers after the dew has dried but before the hot sun has caused them to droop. Most dry in a week or two, depending on the heat in the drying room and the type of flower.

Most flowers should be picked at the peak of bloom or just before. Dried strawflowers look their

Air-dried flowers. From top row to bottom, left to right. *Row one:* goldenrod, red cockscomb, dock, rat-tailed statice; *row two:* sea lavender, artemisia, heather; *row three:* mature Queen Anne's lace, lamb's ears, German statice, pink, white, blue larkspur.

11

Air-dried flowers. From top to bottom, left to right. *Row one:* green hydrangea, baby's breath, cornflower, peegee hydrangea; *row two:* pink cockscomb, pearly everlasting, feverfew; *row three:* honesty, blue salvia, miniature roses, yarrow; *row four:* echinops, roses, natural and bleached teasel, yellow and purple statice.

Unbend one end of a paper clip to make a hook, place one end under the rubber band and the other over the clothesline, with the flowers heads down. Leave enough space between bunches for air to circulate. After the flowers are dried the bunches may be moved closer together to make room for new bunches ready for drying.

Not all flowers dried in the air are hung in bunches. Teasel, dock, and assorted grasses are more easily dried in an upright position. Pussy willow dries best in a warm—not hot—room and takes on graceful curves when placed to dry inside a round container. Some flowers, such as goldenrod, can be hung in bunches, so that straight stems will be available, or placed into baskets to dry, causing them to take on graceful curves.

Drying Flowers in Sand

Many of the flowers used in displays in this book, such as black-eyed-Susans, marigolds, and zinnias, were dried in sand to preserve their original shape. The sand used is sterilized, white play sand, which is available at hardware and toy stores at a reasonable price. Builder's sand is usually damp and not always the finest grade; beach sand contains too many sharp objects, and must be washed and sifted before using it to dry flowers, so considering the low price of play sand, it seems to be the best choice.

Pick the flowers to be sand-dried when they have reached their peak of bloom. Choose a dry day; if that is impossible, pick the flowers and place the stems in a container of very warm water until the moisture on the petals dries. If damp flower heads are placed in the sand the petals will turn brown. If you pick a quantity of flowers at one time, whatever the weather conditions, place all the flowers in warm water so that they will stay fresh until they are to be dried. A limp flower will not dry successfully, nor will one that is beyond its prime.

As with air- and silica-gel-dried flowers, be prepared when sand-drying flowers for some color changes. A few shades of pink will turn lavender, and reds always turn at least two shades darker. If you are looking for a bright red rose, dry Tropicana, or any other orange-red rose. Blues stay true and keep their color well. Yellows dry beautifully but fade faster than other colors to a lovely cream. Unless you have matched some of the yellow flowers to a similar color in the vase you won't be disappointed in the color change.

Flowers should be positioned in sand according to their form. For example, flowers with a relatively flat head and a single row of petals, such as daisies,

best when the center doesn't show. To achieve this, pick the flowers in tight bud, cut the stem, leaving about one inch, insert a 20-gauge green wire about four inches long into the stem or alongside it, and into but not through the base of the flower. As the flower dries it shrinks and grabs the wire tightly. Place the flowers on their wire stems in a container in a warm, not hot, room. They will be dry in four or five days.

Joe-pye-weed and pearly everlasting should also be picked in tight bud. If they are picked when the color is already showing, the flowers will shatter as they dry.

To set up the drying area, string clothesline in rows about two feet apart, crisscrossing the drying room. Cut flowers on long stems, combine them into small bunches of six or eight flowers, and fasten together with rubber bands. As the plants dry, the stems shrink and the rubber bands move with the stems; if string is used, the dried bunches are often found on the floor with the string dangling from the clothesline.

Flowers dried in sand or silica gel. From top row to bottom, left to right. *Row one:* Queen Ann's lace (sand), lily of the valley (silica gel), pompon dahlia (sand), black-eyed Susan (sand); *row two:* off-white rose (silica gel), miniature roses (silica gel), delphinium (sand), tulip (sand); *row three:* miniature rose (silica gel), marigold (sand), dogwood (sand); *row four:* daffodil (silica gel), larkspur (sand), white yarrow (sand), peony (silica gel).

black-eyed Susans, and Queen Anne's lace, are dried face down in the sand. Those with layers of petals, or flowers with an upright shape like roses, carnations, and tulips, should dry face up. Long stalks of flowers, such as delphiniums and sweet peas, are best dried lengthwise, on their sides.

Most of the flowers that are sand-dried will be completely dry in seven to ten days. If it's not possible to remove them from their boxes they can safely stay in the sand indefinitely as long as they are stored in a warm, dry place.

The materials needed for sand-drying are

shoe boxes

wires (20 gauge is the most commonly used)

sterilized play sand

assorted flowers

pen and paper

wire cutters

flower clippers

DRYING HEADS DOWN

This is the easiest method for drying simple flat flowers without a lot of overlapping petals, such as black-eyed Susans.

Cut each flower's stem, leaving about one inch, and insert a four-inch 20-gauge wire into or alongside the stem and slightly into the base of the flower but not through it. As the flower dries it will shrink, gripping the wire and holding it firmly in place. If, for some reason, a wire comes loose from a stem, glue it back into the opening.

Fill a shoe box with an inch or two of dry sand to act as a cushion. Place the wired flowers face down on the sand and cover with another inch or two of sand. (See Figure 1.) Work with one flower at a

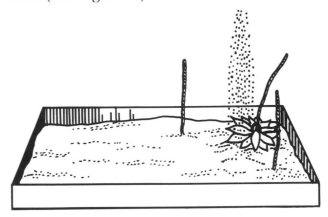

Fig. 1. Sand-drying flowers heads down

time, then proceed with the next flower. The flowers in the box should not be touching. Depending on the size of the box it should hold six to eight flowers. Tuck a piece of paper with the name of the flower and the date in the sand. Place the uncovered box in a warm, dry place. Some flowers need a little extra-special treatment when sand-drying.

Separate dogwood blossoms may be wired and dried face down, but to preserve small branches, bury them in the sand face up.

Pansies are dried face down, and while they do not stand up well to humidity they are useful to embellish potpourri or added to arrangements under glass domes.

Queen Anne's lace keeps its natural look when buried in sand; when air-dried it loses its lovely rounded shape. Since most of these blooms are umbel shaped, a curved place should be scooped out in the sand to receive the rounded head. The stems of Queen Anne's lace are hollow and, once clipped, may be put aside in a box to air-dry. The dried stem can be used to extend a stem of this or another flower if necessary.

Hydrangea should be dried face down, with or without a wire in the stem. Many hydrangea heads are very large and are more useable when broken into smaller blooms. When drying hydrangea, don't let the head of the flower rest on the sand as you cover it, or it will be flattened by the sand being poured over it. Instead, hold the stem with one hand so that the flower is barely touching the sand, while sprinkling more sand carefully in and around the florets. In this manner, the sand serves as a support as well as a drying agent. Blue, pink, and lavender shrub (macrophylla) hydrangea dry best this way. When the flowers left on the plant at the end of the summer turn green they may be air-dried. Peegee hydrangeas, sometimes called snowball bush, may be picked in the fall when the flowers turn green or pink and then air-dried.

During my workshops and lectures, many people say they haven't any luck sand-drying. As I go through the steps with them the reason for the problem surfaces in two areas. One is placing the drying boxes in an unacceptable place, such as a basement (often on the floor), instead of a warm, dry place. A basement can be used as a workroom for drying flowers only if it is equipped with a dehumidifier. The boxes are left uncovered so the warm, dry air in the room can dry out the sand and flowers; if the air in the room is damp the flowers will mildew.

The second reason for failure is drying the wrong flowers. The natural tendency is to dry the flowers available in your garden, which usually means impatiens, which collapse when dried, and/or chrysanthemums, which shatter. Start with the flowers shown in the photographs in this chapter. Once you've enjoyed success with these, experiment. If the experiment doesn't work, don't give up—know it was the flower and not the flower dryer who was at fault.

DRYING HEADS UP

For sand-drying complicated flowers with many petals, the heads-up method is best. These flowers include the carnation, dahlia, hollyhock, nigella, marigold, tulip, and zinnia.

Prepare the flower in the same manner as for drying heads down. The same principle is applied to this method as the first, substituting wire for the stem wherever possible for ease in arranging. Cut the stem, leaving one inch, and insert a four-inch

20-gauge wire up into or alongside the stem, and into but not through the base of the flower.

Place a two-inch cushion of sand in the bottom of the box. Bend the wire stem up and place the flower heads up on the sand so that when the flower is covered the wire will show above the sand. (See Figure 2.) Slowly add the sand, allowing it to build up around the outside of the flower. When the flower is fully supported, sprinkle more sand in and around the petals until the flower is completely covered with an inch or two of sand. Leave the box, uncovered, in a warm, dry place. If care is taken the flower should dry in its original form.

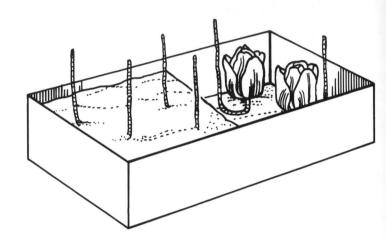

Fig. 2. Sand-drying flowers heads up

Roses are most successfully dried half-opened, although I feel it is worth the gamble to dry fully opened roses if they are fresh. If a petal or two falls off it can be glued back in place with thick white craft glue; if the flower falls apart it can be put in the potpourri box and not be wasted (see Recipe for Potpourri, page 148).

Small tulips should be held in the hand, filled with sand, then placed in a bed of sand at an angle with the wire bending up. Carefully build up the sand around the flower and then completely cover it with sand to a depth of about two inches. Large tulips dry well, but because of their size the petals absorb humidity quickly and droop.

DRYING LENGTHWISE

The best position for drying spiky flowers such as larkspur, delphinium, lilacs, coral bells, and snapdragons is sideways. A shoe box may not be long enough for some of these flowers, so let the length of the flowers determine the length of the box.

Allow a cushion of sand two or three inches deep in the bottom of the box. Do not place the flower on the sand and start pouring sand around it; that can flatten the flower. Instead, hold the flower so that it is slightly touching the top of the sand and sprinkle the sand gently in and around the blossoms. (See Figure 3.) After the sand has been built up around the sides to support the flowers, sprinkle more sand in and around the petals, until the flower is covered with one or two inches of sand.

Most of these flowers will keep their natural stems. If the stem is hollow it may be curved by inserting a wire into it and bending it before placing it in the sand. For ease in removing the flowers once they are dried, place all the heads going in the same direction. As sand is gently poured off it is easier to catch the ends of the stems, rather than take a chance on damaging the flowers.

After the flowers are covered with sand place a paper with the date, name of flower, and an arrow showing which direction the heads are in the box.

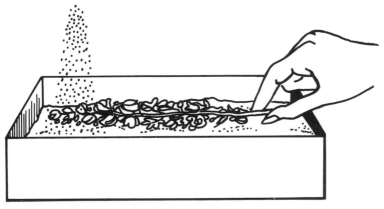

Fig. 3. Sand-drying flowers lengthwise

Drying Flowers in Silica Gel

Silica gel, known as the thirsty chemical, was originally used to absorb moisture in commercially packaged goods. It is now widely used to dry flowers. It is distributed under many names, such as Flower Dri, Mother Nature's Preserves, and Flower Art Silica Gel, and can be found in craft shops, nurseries, flower shops, and supermarkets. It resembles sugar in appearance, and because it is lighter in weight than sand, works better with delicate flowers. Daisies are more likely to keep their petals intact in silica gel; hyacinth florets, wired individually with fine spool wire, dry beautifully, as do lilies of the valley, daffodils, roses, and peonies. But any flowers dried in sand can be dried in silica gel.

The advantages to drying in silica gel are speed

Flowers dried in sand or silica gel. From top row to bottom, left to right. *Row one:* Dutch iris (silica gel), dahlia (silica gel), carnation (sand or silica gel), pink peony (silica gel); *row two:* narcissus (silica gel), zinnia (sand), pink nigella (sand), white nigella (sand), blue nigella (sand), rose (silica gel or sand), ranunculus (silica gel); *row three:* blue hydrangea (sand), zinnia (sand), tulip (sand), rose (sand or silica gel).

and appearance. Most flowers will dry in five days, have more vivid color, and look more lifelike. But the use of silica gel requires a great deal of care and strict attention to the instructions on the package.

Because silica gel absorbs moisture from the air, it is generally held that flowers must be placed in a metal container and sealed airtight after the silica gel has been sprinkled on. If flowers are left in a sealed container of silica gel longer than the specified time, they will often lose their color and turn beige. The loss of color is caused by the heat generated in a tin with the lid on. Because of this possibility of so-called "burning," I use silica gel in the same way as sand: in an uncovered shoe box placed in a warm, dry place, so the silica gel won't absorb moisture and will not generate excessive heat.

Cover each flower with silica gel, as you would sand, either face up, face down, or on its side, depending on its form.

When the drying process is done (about five

15

Preserving leaves and branches. Clockwise, beginning bottom left: perennial ryegrass, broadleaf uniola, holly, pussy willow, Canada wild rye, peony leaf, nandina berries, peony, mountain laurel, eucalyptus.

days), carefully pour off the silica gel and store the flowers in a warm, dry place until they are to be used. Silica-gel-dried flowers will reabsorb moisture from the air and become limp unless they are kept in a low-humidity room. Spraying the flowers with a clear matte fixative (see page 18) before storing them will help protect against humidity.

This drying agent, like sand, can be used over and over again, indefinitely, but because it absorbs moisture from the petals, must be dried before each use. Silica gel has blue crystals added to it in order to gauge its dryness; when the crystals are blue the silica gel is dry, if the crystals are pink, the silica gel is damp. To dry the silica gel place it in a low oven or in the sun for several hours. When not in use, store it in a dry place.

Drying Flowers in a Microwave Oven

If you need to dry a lot of flowers quickly, microwave-drying may be the answer. The same sort of containers used for cooking in a microwave should be used for drying flowers. Remember that the flowers can't be wired when placed in a microwave.

Proceed with the drying process as for drying flowers in silica gel, leaving the container uncovered. Place a glass containing one cup of water in the oven along with the containers filled with flowers and silica gel. Refill the glass as necessary to keep one cup of water.

Dry flowers on medium-high temperature. Timing depends on the type and size of the flowers. Small flowers will take one or two minutes, roses and hydrangeas will take from three to four minutes. If the flowers are left too long they may overdry; if they are not completely dry they may be returned to the oven for another minute. Wait until the container and the silica gel cool down before uncovering or removing the flowers.

Since most of the flowers you dry will probably be from your garden and available to you in the future, keep a log showing the time required for your favorite flowers to dry.

Wires or dried stems may be added to the flower heads with a hot-glue gun. Store the flowers according to the directions for silica-gel-dried flowers.

Preserving Foliage

Most leaves don't dry successfully. They become brittle, and, because they quickly lose their natural color, usually turning beige, they should be sprayed or dyed green. The plant with the most staying power is boxwood. It will dry in the air and stay green for six months or more if kept out of bright light. However, there are two methods of preserving leaves for use in dried arrangements. They are pressing and glycerinizing.

PRESSING

Ferns and many other types of flat leaves can be pressed dry. Make certain the leaves are free of surface moisture. Place a section of newspaper on the floor, position several leaves on the newspaper, then cover with more newspaper. Keep alternating layers of newspaper, and finally weight them down with a stack of books or something equally heavy placed uniformly on top of the papers. Tuck the stack of leaves and newspapers under the bed or in any warm, dry, out-of-the-way place.

The leaves will be dry in 10 to 14 days. When they emerge from the newspapers they will be a lovely shade of green, but if left out in the air they will begin to fade after a few months. To ensure their

Ferns and mosses. From top row to bottom, left to right. *Row one:* assorted pressed ferns; *row two:* reindeer moss, bun moss; *row three:* Spanish moss, dried green sheet moss, Oasis Moss Mate.

Cut the branches between 15 and 24 inches long and either split the stem up about two inches or pound it with a hammer so that it will take up the solution faster. Glycerine is relatively inexpensive and can be purchased at any pharmacy. Most arrangers prepare a solution of one part glycerine to two or three parts very hot water, but I have found that half glycerine and half water gets the best and fastest results. Be sure the water is hot so the glycerine mixes easily and the branches can take up the solution more quickly. Do not put the branches in water first, as that will just dilute the solution as it is absorbed by the stems. Place the stems in a sturdy container with at least six inches of glycerine solution. Check the amount of solution often, adding water as it evaporates. Premixed glycerine and water called "Forever Natural" is available in craft shops.

If the branches are too long, especially thick branches like magnolia, the top leaves will wither before the glycerine solution reaches them. If this

fresh green color lasts longer than that, it is best to spray the leaves with green floral spray. Floral sprays have a matte finish, and are lighter in weight than spray enamels. Moss or avocado green are two good shades to use. Floral sprays are available in craft shops, some hardware stores, and of course flower shops.

Experiment with various types of leaves, such as ferns, peony, rose, and galax, as well as those in your garden. Fall leaves, pressed by the same method, will keep their bright, beautiful colors.

GLYCERINIZING

This process is used to preserve the leaves and branches of large, leafy plants such as apple, beech, flowering crab, forsythia, mountain laurel, and magnolia. Leaves processed in a glycerine solution turn various shades of brown and remain pliable and easy to work with.

The branches to be treated should be picked late in the season when the leaves are full size and the woody stems have matured. If picked too early they are inclined to droop.

Dyed and glycerinized flowers. From top row to bottom, left to right. *Row one:* caspia, German statice, cedar, springerei; *row two:* baby's breath (bleached), pearly everlasting (dip dyed), calamus (spray dyed), pearly everlasting (dip dyed), bloom broom (dyed); *row three:* goldenrod (glycerinized and dip dyed), goldenrod (glycerinized and dip dyed), goldenrod.

happens but the remaining leaves have turned brown, remove the branches from the solution, confine them with a rubber band, and hang them in a warm, dry place. Some of the solution will work its way down through the branch, and any remaining withered leaves can be trimmed. All bottom leaves that might fall into the solution should be removed, along with any damaged or insect-eaten leaves on the stem.

It is possible to purchase individual glycerinized magnolia leaves from florists or nurseries. These can be wired separately and added to arrangements as desired. If you would like to glycerinize your own separate leaves, place the glycerine solution in a flat dish and place the leaves in the solution. If the leaves have a tendency to float, weight them down with stones so they stay under the solution.

Flowers such as goldenrod, bells-of-Ireland, and hydrangea can be glycerinized in the plain solution or with dye added to it. See the dyed flowers on page 17.

As the branches absorb the glycerine, the leaves will become pliable and turn different shades of brown. The processing time varies from branch to branch, but begin checking the progress after about four days. Remove the stems from the solution when they are fully saturated, or they may continue to absorb the solution and the leaves will become sticky. If this happens, the leaves can be cleaned with a damp cloth.

THE CARE AND KEEPING OF DRIED FLOWERS

If plenty of warm, dry storage space is available, it is best to leave bunches of air-dried flowers hanging in place so you can see at a glance what materials you have to work with and be inspired by them. The more fragile flowers dried in sand or silica gel need special care.

After drying and before storing, flowers should be sprayed with a clear matte fixative to protect them from humidity. Krylon clear matte spray is found in most hardware stores, and similar protective sprays are found in art and craft shops, as well as flower shops. (See Sprays, Paints, and Dyes, page 19.) Be sure to get a matte spray; there are some shiny sprays on the market that will give the flowers an artificial look. Two light coats of spray are better than one heavy coat. This should be done outdoors, while wearing a mask to avoid inhaling the fumes. Spraying completed arrangements with clear matte fixative affords additional protection,

especially if individual flowers were not already sprayed.

It is also a good idea to spray dried flowers as protection against infestation, particularly by the cigarette beetle. The eggs of the beetle attach themselves to the flowers, and drying doesn't seem to faze them. The flowers most susceptible are straw-flowers, zinnias, and marigolds. A telltale sign of infestation is a dusting of black powder under an arrangement or when you shake the flower into your hand. If you find a number of flowers in this condition, throw them away so the insects don't attack the rest of the flowers. Treating flowers twice a year with a spray listing pyrethrins first on the can seems to keep the insects under control. Sprays are readily available at garden supply, hardware, or grocery stores.

To store specimen flowers, insert the wire stems into a slice of floral foam or Styrofoam. After they are sprayed against both humidity and insects, place their holder into a box. Spray the inside of the box with insect spray if the flowers are to be stored for some time. Place the boxes in a warm, dry place.

Dried flower arrangements are usually stored during the summer, then brought out to display in the fall. Dried arrangements should only be used when the heat is on in the house and the humidity is low.

TOOLS, EQUIPMENT, AND MECHANICS

The items that go into the flower arranger's kit bag are inexpensive and can be purchased in hardware stores, florist shops, art and craft stores, and floral supply stores.

FLORAL FOAM

This is the material that holds the flowers in place in an arrangement. There are many brands of foam for dried flowers, some harder than others, but the best-known are Sahara and Sahara II, manufactured by the Oasis Company. Sahara is dark brown and strong enough to allow thick stems to penetrate it without breaking, yet easy to cut with a knife. It also holds up well to hot glue. A block is 3 × 4 × 8 inches.

CONTAINERS, BASKETS, AND HOLDERS

Almost any container can be used to hold dried flowers. Just be sure it is in proportion to your planned arrangement. Plain papier-mâché vases of

Floral mechanics. Clockwise, beginning bottom left: flat wicker wall basket, paper ribbon, raffia, papier-mâché florist containers, basket, straw wreath, wire wreath frame.

various sizes, such as florists use, can be placed inside more decorative containers, or wrapped in paper ribbon as shown on page 37. Baskets are especially compatible with preserved flowers, and have the added advantage of coming in many sizes and shapes. Clear vases pose a problem for the dried flower arranger, because the unattractive dried stems show through. But even this can be overcome with a coat of paint on the inside (see the vases on page 40).

Bouquets require a special holder, like the one in the photo on the right. A holder allows the bouquet to be completed over time. You can add a few flowers, then put it down to finish later. A nosegay made in the hand can't be put down and picked up again without the flowers shifting position. The plastic bouquet holders are filled with floral foam for either fresh or dried flowers. White and off-white lace collars are available in a variety of sizes to fit the holders, which come in two sizes: 3¾ inches in diameter and 2½ inches in diameter. The smaller size, called Junior Miss, was used for the nosegays on pages 112 and 115 and the bouquet on top of the wedding cake on page 93. An even smaller flower holder is the wrist corsage holder, shown in the photo on the right and in Figure 30 on page 86, and used in the ribbon arch on page 87.

The mechanic used for decorating candleholders is called an O'dapter™ and is made by the Oasis Company. (See Figure 27 on page 64.) The rubber tip of the O'dapter fits into the candlestick; above that is the hard green plastic flower holder, which is filled with foam; the candle is inserted into the foam and flowers are added to surround it. An O'dapter was used in the decorated candlestick on page 65.

Bouquet holders and collars. From top to bottom: hand-held bouquet holder, wrist corsage holder with lace collar, lace collar for hand-held bouquet holder.

SPRAYS, PAINTS, AND DYES

All flowers dried in sand or silica gel should be sprayed with clear matte fixative to protect them from humidity. Sturdier air-dried flowers also benefit from being sprayed. (See The Care and Keeping of Dried Flowers, page 18.)

Avoid glossy sprays; they give the flowers an artificial look. Use a clear matte spray fixative, such as Krylon, which is sold in hardware and paint stores; Design Master Super Surface Sealer is available in flower and craft shops; and clear matte sprays commonly used as a fixative for charcoal drawings can be found in art-supply stores.

Spray paint of any kind should only be used outdoors. Wear a mask and choose a warm, calm day. It is best to give the flowers or the arrangements two light coats of spray rather than one heavy one.

Color is often added to dried flowers to perk them up if they fade, when a special color scheme is needed, or to recapture the green color of leaves. The quickest and easiest way to add color is to use spray paints especially designed for dried flowers. They are available in craft shops, nurseries, and flower shops in a wide variety of colors. All-purpose spray paints labeled "matte" can also be used. To achieve very deep colors, use a concentrated plant dye, such as Floralife Dip and Rinse, which can be purchased from a florist or floral supply company. Follow the directions on the container. Dipping the dried flowers in a concentrated solution of fabric dye is another way of adding color to flowers such as statice, caspia, goldenrod, baby's breath, and sea lavender.

GLUES AND CLAY

When decorating containers or arrangements with ribbons and bows, birds, butterflies, or strings of pearls you must know which glue to use. Flower arrangers use both hot glue from a glue gun and thick white craft glue.

If the material to be glued is heavy, such as a big flower or a loop of ribbon, it is best to use hot glue from a glue gun because the glue dries so quickly there is no need to hold the material in place during the drying process. If you are looping a string of pearls around a basket handle, glue the pearls here and there to the handle with a hot-glue gun. However, if you are adding single pearls to an arrangement, use thick craft glue to hold them in place, because the individual pearls aren't heavy and when using small items such as pearls there is a danger of burning your fingers with the hot glue. Stems should be added to flowers dried in the microwave with a hot-glue gun rather than with slower-drying craft glue.

Hot-glue guns are available in hardware and department stores, in craft shops, and from florist supply companies. The gun should have a trigger mechanism and a holder to rest the gun in when not in active use. Buy the best glue sticks available. A danger of working with a glue gun is the possibility of burns. There is less chance of mishap if the glue is applied to the larger object instead of the smaller. For instance, when gluing flowers onto a basket, place the glue on the basket and press the flowers into the glue.

Strings, or cobwebs, of glue are a problem caused by the hot glue hitting the cooler air. When working with sturdy air-dried flowers a hair dryer can be turned on the strings to melt them. But the rush of air from the dryer might damage delicate flowers.

Tools and equipment. From top row to bottom, left to right. *Row one:* floral foam for dried flowers, plastic pot scrubber closed and opened, fine spool wire, Davee tape, floral clay in tape form; *row two:* hot-glue gun and glue sticks, Velverette thick white craft glue in tube and jar, Alene's thick white craft glue, floral tape, hard plastic candle pick, chenille (pipe cleaner); *row three:* clippers (also called pruners), knife for cutting foam, needle-nose pliers, pole pins (also called fern pins), 18-inch lengths of 20-gauge wire.

Thick white craft glue, with the consistency of cake frosting, is better for working with dried flowers and decorative trims than all-purpose household glue, which is too thin. Three brands that have proven to be successful are Velverette, Bond Number 527 Craft Cement, and Aleene's Thick Designer Tacky Glue. All of these glues dry clear. Craft glue takes longer to dry than hot glue but is a better choice when gluing delicate flowers such as baby's breath or small flowers like the globe amaranth glued to the Mother Bear on page 160. These glues are available in craft shops.

Floral clay, such as Cling, is sold in flower shops and floral supply stores. Although it is still sold in squares, it is also available in strips separated by paper, and this form is very easy to use. Just pull off a ribbon of clay the size you need to fit inside the rim of your container and position it. Then press the floral foam into the clay for a secure fit. Clay can also be used to attach decorations to containers.

TAPES AND WIRES

The tape used to hold floral foam in place (see page 27) is Davee tape, commonly used by florists, or adhesive tape, which it closely resembles. It is a little stickier than adhesive tape and is used by florists for wet as well as dry arrangements. For arrangers of dried flowers, adhesive tape works well and is found in most households. For small arrangements split the adhesive tape lengthwise to a width of ¼ inch.

Floral tape is used for binding wire to short stems to extend them, as described on page 21. It is made of stretchy paper impregnated with a sticky substance that allows it to cling to a wire, stem, or itself. It comes in many colors, the most useful of which are green, brown, and white. Floral tape can be purchased in craft and flower shops.

The green wire used in drying flowers can be purchased in craft shops, flower shops, or hardware stores. The most useful thickness for substitute stems is 20 gauge, which is generally sold in 18-inch lengths. Green is my preferred color because it is most natural looking and does not rust if it is exposed to water. The larger the wire's gauge number, the finer the wire. Very fine spool wire is sometimes found in 30 or 32 gauge. If glue is not available, fine wire can be used to attach ribbons to baskets, but it is difficult to hide the wire, and "mechanics" should never show.

It is very often necessary to artificially extend a flower's stem, either because the original stem broke or because most flowers are dried with three- or four-inch wire stems. To lengthen a stem, cut a hollow stem (some stems are hollow when fresh, others become hollow when they dry—save stems from flowers you pick) or a piece of 20-gauge wire to the desired length. Slip the hollow stem over the short stem or overlap the original stem and the new wire by one to two inches. Attach floral tape close under the flower and wrap it around the stem, overlapping it as you move down. (See Figure 4.) Make the stem long enough that you can add the flower to an arrangement without damaging other flowers.

Thick, fuzzy pipe cleaners called chenilles, which are available in craft stores or flower shops, are used to attach flower arrangements to chairs, banisters, and so forth. See, for example, the Christmas garland on page 115. Chenilles are available in white, green, red, and various other colors.

Paper-covered wire twist ties (which come with plastic food and garbage bags to close them) are also versatile for attaching flower arrangements to

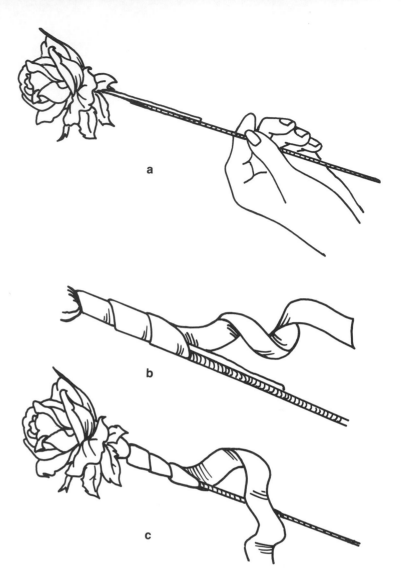

Fig. 4. Extending a stem with wire and floral tape

furniture or to artificial garlands. They can often be used in place of chenilles.

Nylon filament, or fishing line, is used to secure moss to floral foam on wreath or topiary frames.

BASES AND FRAMES

Wreaths. Wreaths need support, which can be furnished in various ways. Wire wreath frames are circular or heart-shaped (see Figure 5 on the following page), come in a variety of sizes, and are available in craft shops, nurseries, and flower shops. They are made concave with three or four wire supports that allow them to be filled with foam so flowers can be inserted vertically, showing the blossom in full flower. A wreath made on a wire frame is quickly and easily put together. The wire frame itself is used for hanging.

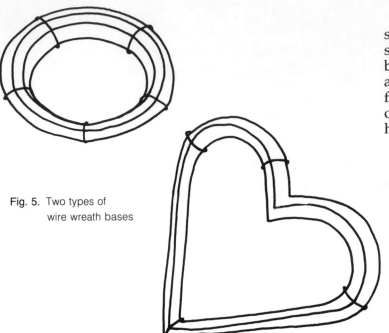

Fig. 5. Two types of wire wreath bases

Round straw wreath bases are available in many sizes and can be dampened and formed into oval shapes if desired. The wreath, formed of straw bound together with nylon cord, is available in craft and flower shops, as well as in supermarkets where flowers are sold. Dried flowers can be glued directly onto the wreath or attached to it in small bunches held in place with pole pins.

Fig. 7. Inserting a flower vertically into a moss-covered wire wreath base

A 10-inch-diameter wreath requires one block of floral foam to form the base for the flowers. Slice a block of floral foam in half as shown in Figure 6. Push one half block of floral foam into the open side of the wire wreath frame hard enough to make an indentation. Then cut along the curved lines and place inside the frame. Repeat with the second half block of foam. Use the leftover pieces to fill in the empty spaces.

Wrap Spanish moss around the frame and secure it with nylon filament (fishing line), which will hold the foam and moss in place. (See Figure 7.)

Pole, or fern, pins are shaped like squared-off hair pins made of stainless steel. They are available in various lengths in craft and flower shops. Buy the shortest length possible for ease in inserting into the wreath frame.

You will generally have to add a hanger to a straw wreath frame. Unwrap the green plastic from the frame. Bring a 12-inch piece of 20-gauge wire inside the wreath and back out, then twist the two ends together. Wind the wire around your finger to form a circle to be used as a hanger and then wind the ends around the wire at the beginning of the circle. (See Figure 8.) Push the ends of the wire into the straw so they won't scratch the wall. Very strong ribbon could also be used as a hanger.

Styrofoam wreath frames can be used but only if they have wire reinforcements in the center. Otherwise they might split. Solid Styrofoam forms such as the heart are stronger and ideal for the valentine on page 121.

In some dried flower arrangements, especially if the flower stems are heavy or the floral foam is inserted vertically (see arrangements on pages 34, 36, and 46), it is necessary to reinforce the foam. Chicken wire is commonly used for this purpose, but it is not easy to master. The easiest way I've found is to use a plastic mesh pot scrubber or a plastic mesh vegetable bag, both of which are available in supermarkets.

Fig. 6. Cutting foam for a wire wreath base (left); foam-filled wire wreath base

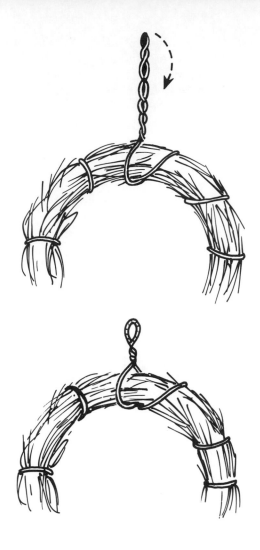

Fig. 8. Making a wire hanger for a straw wreath

To use a pot scrubber, first turn it inside out, forming a tube, and pull on it horizontally to stretch it. Cut the foam to fit the vase, then pull the pot scrubber over it. Close the opening at the top with a pole pin or piece of bent wire. The mesh will also hold more than one piece of foam together. Flowers are pushed through the holes in the mesh. If the holes are too small to accommodate a stem, they can be cut; the mesh will not "run." Figure 17 on page 34 shows how a pot scrubber is used in an arrangement.

Topiary base. The dazzling display of flowers crowning a long potted stem of a topiary tree needs a strong supporting base. Although the size of the base depends on the size of the trunk used, the basic topiary unit requires the following materials:

plaster of Paris

water

plastic foam cup or similar container, 3″ in diameter × 3½″ high

woody stem for trunk

⅓ block Sahara floral foam

Spanish moss

nylon filament (fishing line)

container for finished arrangement, e.g., papier-mâché, 5″ in diameter × 4″ high

measuring cup and spoon

hot-glue gun and glue sticks

knife

wire cutters

Following the directions on the plaster of Paris container, mix a small amount of water and plaster in the plastic cup. (After much experimenting it was found that mixing the plaster of Paris and making the topiary base in the same container cuts down on a lot of mess and guesswork.) The plastic cup should be at least two-thirds filled with the plaster mixture. Immediately insert the trunk of the topiary into the center of the plaster of Paris. Hold it for a minute or two so it remains straight, then set it aside to dry thoroughly.

Cover the ⅓ block of floral foam with Spanish moss, then wind nylon filament (fishing line) around and around it to hold the moss in place and reinforce the foam.

Some arrangers use a Styrofoam ball for a topiary top, but it is very difficult to push flower stems into the hard Styrofoam. If you do use Styrofoam, glue everything in place.

When the plaster is thoroughly dry, attach the top to the tree trunk. Indent a spot in the floral foam for the tree trunk to enter, apply hot glue there, then gently push the foam down on top of the trunk. Allow the glue to set. If the topiary seems wobbly, turn it upside down and apply glue all around the spot where the trunk and floral foam meet.

This is the topiary base, as shown in Figure 9 on the following page.

Place the topiary base inside the arrangement container. Use stuffing (newspaper, plastic bags, etc.) under and around the cup to steady it as necessary. Cover the top of the container with Spanish

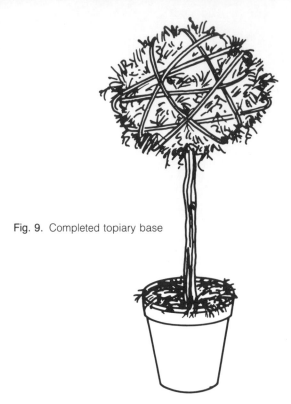

Fig. 9. Completed topiary base

moss, leaves, sheet moss, or any other appropriate material to hide the mechanics. (See photo below.)

MOSSES

A variety of mosses are used either to enhance an arrangement, as the bun moss does the bouquet

on page 123, or to decorate a basket, as shown on page 136. Most often dried green sheet moss or Spanish moss give an arrangement a finished look by hiding the floral foam so it won't be seen between the flowers. Packages of the dried mosses mentioned here are available in craft shops, nurseries, and flower shops.

Bun moss is rounded, green, and velvety, and can be dug up from your yard or purchased from a florist. If you air-dry it, keep in mind that like all greens it will fade and will need to be sprayed with green paint or dip-dyed in green dye.

Reindeer moss is a light gray dried moss useful for giving a light touch to wreaths and arrangements that need a variety of textures. It can be purchased in flower shops and nurseries.

Gray and fluffy-looking Spanish moss is commonly used to hide floral foam. In its dried form it is available in craft and flower shops, as well as nurseries.

Another moss used to hide floral foam is dried green sheet moss. It can also be applied as decoration on the edges of baskets or cover them completely. This moss is also available in craft shops, flower shops, and nurseries.

Oasis® Moss Mate™ is a plastic sheet with short pieces of green moss bonded to it. Since it is very thin and pliable, without the sticks and soil that sometimes cling to dried sheet moss, it is useful for craft projects. It is available in craft and flower shops. The gift basket on page 131 shows how Moss Mate can be used.

CUTTERS, CLIPPERS, AND PLIERS

The basic cutting tools needed for making flower arrangements are probably already in your home tool box. If not, they can be bought at any hardware store. Clippers, sometimes called pruners, are used to cut flower stems and branches. Wire cutters are needed for cutting lengths of green florist wire to make substitute stems. Needle-nose pliers are used to insert flowers into almost-completed arrangements and can also double as wire cutters. Also handy to have are a scissor for cutting ribbons, fabric, and other thin items; a steak knife for cutting floral foam; and a plastic knife for spreading glue.

RIBBONS, BOWS, AND EMBELLISHMENTS

All of these items enhance a dried arrangement as much as the proper container. Ribbons may be made of fabric or paper, formed into bows and loops. Other embellishments may be birds, bird's nests, butterflies, strings of pearls, or small bunches of grapes.

When paper ribbon was introduced just a few years ago it took the flower and craft worlds by storm. It is easy to work with, inexpensive, comes in a rainbow of colors, sizes, and widths, and is available in most craft and floral supply shops. It has established itself as a necessary part of a flower arranger's basic equipment.

Paper ribbon complements dried flowers because of its muted colors and matte finish. It has a "country" look, but can look elegant and formal as well. Wrapped and tied in a bow it can dress up a plain papier-mâché container or turn a simple basket arrangement into something spectacular. (See arrangements on pages 37, 80, and 85 as examples.)

The ribbon comes in either 4- or 8-inch widths and 6- or 12-yard lengths, twisted, semi-untwisted, and completely untwisted. Most often it comes twisted. Cut it into shorter lengths before using so it will be easier to untwist. When untwisted it has the look of cornhusks. It can be ironed if a smoother look is desired, but the lines will remain. Some paper ribbon is stiffer than others and therefore more difficult to untwist. When this is the case, dip it into a bowl of water (don't soak it) or run it under a faucet, and it will be much easier to untwist.

To cover a papier-mâché container, cut paper ribbon into the length required to cover your container vertically (down one side, across the bottom, and up the other side), plus two inches. Untwist it as necessary. Use a hot-glue gun to apply a line of glue about one inch inside the container, then press the paper into the glue. Run another line of glue just under the outside rim, press paper into it, and allow this to dry for a few seconds. Then bring the paper down under the bottom of the container and up the other side. Apply glue under the rim and one inch inside the container and press the paper into the glue. Glue the second strip next to the first, and so on. The number of strips needed will depend upon the size of the container and the width of the paper. Figure 10 illustrates the process. One-inch strips of paper can be glued horizontally under the rim as a finishing touch. Bows can be added with hot glue as desired.

To make a bow from paper ribbon cut one piece of untwisted paper ribbon 20 inches long for the bow and one 24 inches long for the tie. After untwisting the ribbon, fold one end of the bow under the other, squeeze it together in the middle, and wrap the tie around it, tying it in a knot. Puff up the bow and smooth out the streamers; notch the ends if desired. (See Figures 11A and 11B.)

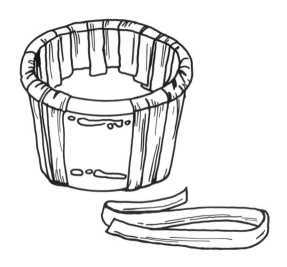

Fig. 10. Covering a container with paper ribbon

a

b

Fig. 11. Making a bow with paper ribbon

Fig. 12. Making a bow and streamers with fabric ribbon

Satin ribbon is very popular, adding shine to otherwise dull decorations, but the shiny look in wide widths overpowers dried flower arrangements. Very narrow satin ribbon or grosgrain works with the arrangement instead of against it. Lace ribbon is delicate and lovely, and perfect for wedding flower arrangements.

Making a bow of fabric ribbon is similar to making one of paper ribbon. Fold the ends of the bow under one another (Figure 12A), securing the ribbon in the center between thumb and forefinger, and make one, two, or three overlapping folds (Figure 12B). Place a single piece of ribbon over the center folds and tie in a knot (Figure 12C).

This type of bow is often attached to a basket handle with hot glue. When the bow is to decorate the base of the handle it can be attached by slipping a wire through the knot, hairpinlike, then inserting it into the floral foam.

A bow with streamers can be made the same way, but before tying, any number of ribbons can be placed under the bow, and then tied as shown in Figure 12D.

GUIDELINES FOR ARRANGING DRIED FLOWERS

The reason for making a dried flower arrangement determines the size, type, and number of flowers and the container to be used. There is no one way to go about planning an arrangement. If you have a lovely vase you want to feature, start there, if you have an abundance of one kind of flower, let that be your inspiration. If you want to make an arrangement of mixed garden flowers because you have a plentiful supply, start there. If you plan to give the arrangement to a friend, keep her taste in mind, and where she might place the flowers. A centerpiece makes a welcome addition to a dining room table because it dresses it up when not in use and can be used for dinner parties as well. To make sure the arrangement is coordinated with her china and decorating scheme, ask your friend if she has a container for you to fill.

Almost any container can be used to hold dried flowers, since there is no concern about the vase holding water. Silver containers, however, are not a good choice, not because of the silver itself but because it needs polishing. Make the arrangement planned for a silver container in a papier-mâché or similar holder that will fit into the silver one, to be removed easily when the silver needs polishing.

Select a container that will complement your planned arrangement. Baskets are wonderful filled with dried flowers. They can be painted or left natural; a large basket can sit on the floor filled with tall spiky flowers; a small basket can be filled with delicate specimen flowers and placed on a side-table. If the basket is light in weight, tall, or has a rounded bottom, it should be weighted down to keep it from tipping over. Stones or something equally heavy will serve as ballast to substitute for the weight that water furnishes in fresh flower arrangements.

Once you're confident the basket won't tip over, add the floral foam that will hold the flowers in place. Measure the foam for the container by placing it over the rim as shown in Figure 13. Push

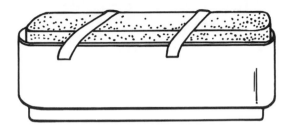

Fig. 14. Taping floral foam, which rises ½ inch above rim of container

Fig. 13. Measuring floral foam to fit container

down on the foam, making an indentation to serve as a cutting guide. Using a dull steak knife, trim away the excess foam and push the shaped piece into the container. The foam should fit into the container as snugly as possible, rising at least ½ inch above the rim, allowing stiff stems to be inserted at an angle in order to give them a curved appearance. Tape the foam securely to the container to ensure that it stays in place. (See Figure 14.) Do not criss-cross the center with tape; that is space needed for the important center flower. Davee tape is customarily used by florists for securing foam because it is extra strong and can be used for wet as well as dry arrangements. Adhesive tape can be used also. Cut the tape in half lengthwise and tape it about one inch over the edge of the container. If the tape

shows white over a dark container, color it with a marking pen.

Once the foam is securely in place, cover it with Spanish moss, dried green moss, or short pieces of filler flowers such as goldenrod, German statice, or hydrangea. Use enough—the foam and tape should never show through an arrangement.

If the arrangement is to be viewed from all sides, the vase should be turned often while the design is in progress to make certain it will be symmetrical. To facilitate this, place the vase on a lazy Susan, such as the kind used in kitchen cupboards.

The height of the arrangement should be approximately twice the height of the container. Always start with tall, spiky flowers to serve as guidelines for maximum height and arrangement shape. (See Figure 15.) Stay inside this outline once established, except for the addition of delicate grasses. Follow your spiky outline flowers with air-dried filler ma-

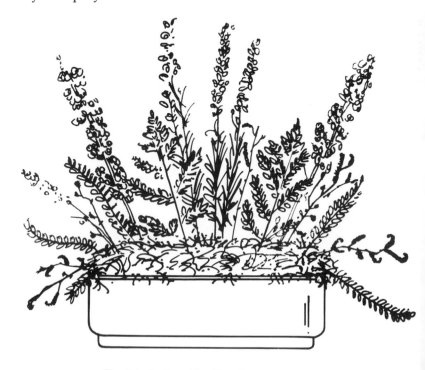

Fig. 15. Outline of traditional arrangement

27

terial in different lengths for variety. Then add rounded air-dried flowers, placing some deep into the arrangement. The sand- or silica-gel-dried flowers are added next for the greatest impact and also because they are the most delicate. If baby's breath is used it should be the last flower added; break off short pieces, dip the ends in craft glue, and place here and there in the arrangement. Remember that two or three times more dried flowers than fresh will be needed to make a beautiful bouquet, so have on hand twice as many dried flowers as you think you will need.

Traditional arrangements should have a vertical central stem, with all other stems radiating at an angle from that. (See Figure 15.) Guard against placing large or specimen flowers directly opposite each other, marching two by two, giving the arrangement a stiff, artificial look. Instead, visualize a ribbon of color running through the arrangement and follow that.

The addition of some yellow or white flowers brightens dried arrangements. The Victorians felt that every flower arrangement should have some yellow in it because most flowers contain some yellow in their centers.

Flowers needn't be used in the form in which they are dried or purchased. A full branch of German statice would be difficult to place in a half-finished arrangement, but if it is broken up into short pieces and taped to a wire stem it will be more useful. (See Figures 16A, 16B.) Large flower heads,

such as cockscomb and hydrangea, will take to the same treatment with equally good results.

Often, large bunches of purchased dried caspia, baby's breath, and German statice break up badly if they are pulled apart without first misting or dampening them slightly. After gently separating the stems, form them into smaller bunches and allow them to dry before putting them into an arrangement.

Air-dried roses can be forced open a little more by holding them over steam and gently opening them with a toothpick as they become slightly softened.

To add fragrance to a bouquet, sprinkle it with dried lavender, mint blossoms, or other fragrant flowers.

Dried flower arrangements should be stored during the summer months because the humidity will cause the flowers to droop and fade. Recipients of floral gifts should be told that dried flower arrangements should be displayed only when the house is heated and humidity is not a problem.

With care dried flower arrangements will last a year, sometimes two, but after that it is time to break up some of the petals for potpourri (see page 148), throw the others away, and save the sturdy material to be used again. If a bouquet is displayed in one place for a long time, it is taken for granted and its beauty no longer appreciated. If an arrangement becomes dusty it's time to replace it.

Designing Wedding Displays and Bridal Flowers

Wedding arrangements made from dried flowers offer the practicality of being made well in advance of the big day and the pleasure of keeping them long after the event. The Wedding Flowers chapter (see pages 67–94) contains many beautiful displays, but before attempting any, consider the following.

THE BRIDAL PARTY FLOWERS

There is little doubt that the bride is the star of the show and that the role of the bridesmaids is to be decorative, adding color and beauty to the ceremony and enhancing that of the bride.

When choosing the flowers for the bridal bouquet, it is important not only to include the bride's favorite flowers but to make certain the bouquet is neither overpowering nor too small. This potential problem can be solved by having the bride pose with loops of ribbon the approximate size of the

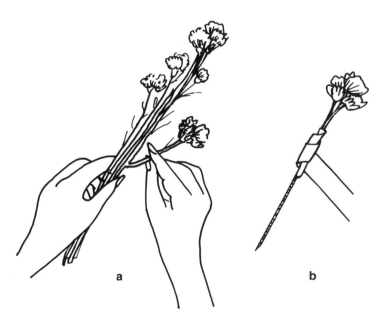

a   b

Fig. 16. Taping short flower pieces to a wire stem

bouquet, adding or subtracting at will. In this way you can judge the most flattering size for the bouquet. The same should be done for the maid of honor. It is difficult to decide the size for each bridesmaid so a middle road is best, as represented by the nosegays on pages 76–78. The plastic handles of bouquet holders should be covered with white floral tape and then wrapped in white satin ribbon to prevent slipping and to give the bouquet a finished look.

If the bride chooses to wear a hat, the design should reflect the colors and textures in her bouquet.

The groom's boutonniere, as well as those of the best man and ushers, should always be made of fresh flowers. One enthusiastic hug would cause a dried flower boutonniere to shatter. Choose traditional boutonniere flowers, such as stephanotis, rose buds, or lilies of the valley, or select blossoms that complement the bridal bouquets.

Flower girls are sometimes very young and find it difficult to manage a basket filled with flowers, but a lightweight half basket covered with paper ribbon and trimmed with equally lightweight flowers is pretty, practical, and easy to carry. A flower-bedecked hat is sometimes a better choice than to try to arrange flowers in a young child's fine hair.

DECORATING THE CHURCH

Flowers decorating the church should complement the style of the church as well as reflect the beauty of the bouquets carried by the wedding party.

The accent or specimen flowers in church arrangements should be large so they can be seen from a distance. The peonies in the pedestal arrangement on page 30 are a good example.

In altar arrangements be sure your outline and filler flowers are dense enough that the church wall, whether stone or wood, does not show through and interfere with the design.

Often the church has vases that are traditionally used. If so, measure them in advance so your containers can be fitted inside them. Most pedestals will hold a 6-inch container comfortably.

DECORATING THE HOME OR HALL

Flower-filled baskets can be used as a substitute for hanging green plants. Paper ribbon is perfect for covering inexpensive baskets since the dull matte finish of paper ribbon complements perfectly the subdued colors of dried flowers. The color scheme of the bridal party bouquets and table decorations can be carried into the hanging baskets.

A unique decoration that will enhance the overall effect of the room decorations is the addition of an oversized paper ribbon bow to festoon the archway

or doorway through which the bridal party will make their entrance. A wreath is always a welcome sight, and conjures up the vision expressed by the phrase "wreathed in smiles," especially on a wedding day. The flowers used on a bridal wreath can be the same as the blossoms in the bridal bouquet.

The wedding table can feature a basket centerpiece in the bridal colors flanked by the bridal party bouquets (placed in weighted vases) and baskets. A similar, smaller centerpiece, containing delightful favors, can grace the guests' table.

The cake, on a separate table, can be beautifully decorated with a floral wreath and a nosegay. Surrounding the cake with a wreath is not only pretty but practical since it is less likely to be damaged than a wreath on the edge of the table. A small nosegay decorating the cake top is a true keepsake and a reminder of the wedding day, as many couples freeze the top of the cake to be eaten on their first anniversary.

Table Displays & Centerpieces

Dried flower arrangements can enhance and reflect the colors in a particular room. Coffee tables are made interesting, hall tables colorful, and buffets cheerier with the addition of flower arrangements no matter what the season.

A dried flower arrangement as a dining table centerpiece should be no more than 15 inches high. You should be able to see over it, and it should be attractive from all sides as well as from above.

Because of their muted colors, dried flowers may be mixed without fear of colors clashing. However, most shades of blue do not show up well under artificial light, an exception being the bright blue of hydrangea.

Elegant Mauve

This blend of pink, mauve, and maroon flowers creates a glowing combination of colors reflected in its brass container. This one-sided arrangement would be a welcome remembrance of summer next to a wall that's in need of some brightening.

FLOWERS & FOLIAGE

Air-dried

heather (10 deep pink)

cockscomb (12 pink)

German statice (28)

caspia (20 natural, 24 dyed mauve)

larkspur (20 pink)

strawflowers (15 white)

baby's breath (15)

Miscellaneous

silica-gel-dried roses (18 maroon)

glycerinized eucalyptus (17)

Spanish moss

SIZE

Finished arrangement is 24″ wide × 19″ high.

MATERIALS

brass container, 10″ long × 5″ wide × 4″ high

1½ blocks floral foam

Davee or adhesive tape

thick white craft glue

clear matte spray fixative

knife

clippers

needle-nose pliers

INSTRUCTIONS

1. Read The Basics of Preserving and Arranging, pages 10–30.

2. Place one half block of floral foam (cut lengthwise) in the bottom of the container. Place a whole block on top of that, rising ½ inch above the rim, and tape into place (see page 27). Cover with Spanish moss.

3. Using the photograph as a guide, place the eucalyptus branches to form the outline. Add pink larkspur, followed by the other spiky dried flowers such as heather and caspia. Work from the back to the front placing the same flowers with shorter stems as shown in the photograph. Add white strawflowers and maroon roses as shown. Dip the stems of baby's breath into glue before placing them here and there in the arrangement to add light and interest.

This display is arranged like the centerpiece on page 52 but with the center flower and those next to it placed in the back of the arrangement, which makes it perfect to place against a wall.

4. Spray with clear matte fixative (see page 19).

Blue and Green

To produce the two colors in this arrangement the blue hydrangeas, which bloomed during the summer months, were dried in sand; the green hydrangeas were hung in the attic to dry in the air after they had turned green.

FLOWERS & FOLIAGE

air-dried hydrangeas (20 green)

sand-dried hydrangeas (20 blue)

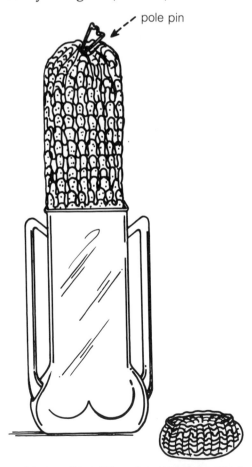

Fig. 17. Pot scrubber used to reinforce foam inserted vertically

SIZE

Finished arrangement is 20" wide × 27" high.

MATERIALS

antique metal vase, 4" in diameter × 10" high

rocks or stones for weight

1 block floral foam

plastic mesh pot scrubber

strip of floral clay

clear matte spray fixative

knife

clippers

needle-nose pliers

INSTRUCTIONS

1. Read The Basics of Preserving and Arranging, pages 10–30.

2. Before starting the actual arrangement, fill the bottom of the vase with rocks or stones to weight it down. The floral foam must fit vertically, rising 7 inches above the rim of the container. Measure and trim the foam, round off the top corners, then set it aside. Push a strip of floral clay inside the vase around the rim.

3. Because of the heavy stems and its vertical rise, the foam should be reinforced with a plastic mesh pot scrubber (see page 23 and Figure 17).

Situate the reinforced foam correctly in the vase, pushing it into the clay.

4. Arrange the green hydrangeas first, following the photograph, then add the blue. Give the back a finished look by filling in with flowers that did not dry as successfully as those in the front.

5. Spray with clear matte fixative (see page 19).

Bright and Beautiful

The color of the paper ribbon surround- ing a simple papier-mâché holder sets the tone for this dramatic floral bouquet. The wild grasses from Texas teamed with garden variety hydrangea, red roses, and bloom broom complement one another in a surprising way. This handsome arrange- ment would be ideal sitting on a pedestal adding color to a dull corner.

FLOWERS & FOLIAGE 🌿

Air-dried

money plants (7)

roses (30 red)

baby's breath (20)

hydrangeas (20 green)

Canada wild rye (15)

perennial ryegrass (15)

broadleaf uniola (15)

Miscellaneous

bloom broom (15 small bunches, dyed red)

glyerinized eucalyptus (14)

SIZE

Finished arrangement is 30″ wide × 27″ high.

MATERIALS

papier-mâché, holder 6″ wide × 9″ high

stones or rocks for weight

1½ blocks floral foam

plastic pot scrubber

strip of floral clay

4 yds. dark red paper ribbon 8″ wide

thick white craft glue

clear matte spray fixative

clippers

scissors

hot-glue gun and glue sticks

needle-nose pliers

INSTRUCTIONS

1. Read The Basics of Preserving and Arranging, pages 10–30.

2. Untwist the paper ribbon and follow the di- rections on page 25 to cover the container with paper ribbon. Make a double bow according to directions on page 26. Cut a piece of paper rib- bon 20 inches long for the top bow, and one 24 inches long for the bottom bow. The tie is 24 inches long before tying. Tie the bow, puff up the loops, and hot-glue to the vase.

3. Place rocks or stones in the bottom of the con- tainer to weight it down. Stick a piece of floral clay all around the inside top of the vase.

4. Because of the size of the container and ar- rangement, the floral foam is placed vertically into the container. Whenever this is done, the foam should be strengthened with a plastic mesh pot scrubber or a mesh vegetable bag.

First cut 1 block of floral foam in half length- wise, put the full block and the half block to-

gether, and trim to fit the vase. Follow the directions for using a pot scrubber on page 23.

Place the reinforced blocks of foam vertically in the vase, forcing them at least 4 inches below the rim, and press into the floral clay (see Figure 17 on page 34).

5. Use Figure 15 on page 27 and the photograph as a guide to creating the outline. The basic outline material was eucalyptus, filled in with grasses, followed by green hydrangeas on the sides and front. The remainder of the flowers were added, finishing with the roses and baby's breath. Longer stems of baby's breath than usual are used in this one-sided arrangement, but the stems are still dipped into glue first. If stems are not long enough, extend them with wire and tape (see page 21).

6. Spray with clear matte fixative (see page 19).

Painted Ladies

Simple, inexpensive glass rose bowls have been turned into colorful containers just by adding a little paint. The flowers in these related pieces reflect the colors in the decorated vases. Any round glass container, such as a goldfish bowl, can be painted the same way.

FLOWERS & FOLIAGE

Air-dried

larkspur (14 pink, 14 white, 18 blue)

caspia (28)

globe amaranth (16 pink, 16 white)

statice (10 blue)

German statice (1 medium bunch)

pearly everlasting (8 dyed rose)

Miscellaneous

sand-dried yarrow (6 white)

glycerinized goldenrod (10 dyed red)

springerei, stems (24 treated and dyed green)

SIZE

Finished large arrangement is 14" wide × 16" high.

Finished small arrangement is 9" wide × 10" high.

MATERIALS

2 rose bowls, 1 6" in diameter × 5½" high and 1 4" in diameter × 3½" high.

1½ blocks floral foam

Davee or adhesive tape

acrylic craft paints: white, red, green, blue

clear matte spray fixative

knife

clippers

needle-nose pliers

INSTRUCTIONS

1. Read The Basics of Preserving and Arranging, pages 10–30.

2. Paint the vases at least a day or two before making the arrangements, to allow time for the paint to dry. Pour a small amount of paint into the bowl, allowing it to run down one side, across the bottom and, by turning it upside down, up the other (see Figure 18). Allow time for the paint to set between colors, although interesting colors result when paints are allowed to combine. No paints were combined before they were used on these vases. The overlapping of red and white inside the bowl produced the pink seen in the smaller vase. Pour in the paint and move the bowl around so that the entire inside surface is covered. Turn the bowl upside down over newspapers to catch the runoff. Allow the bowls to dry upright completely before using them.

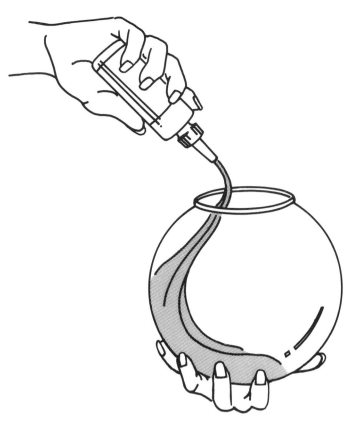

Fig. 18. Painting a clear glass bowl

3. Fill the bowls with floral foam, allowing it to rise ½ inch above the rim, and tape in place (see page 27).

4. Add short stems of German statice to cover the foam, making a small arrangement to build on. Use pink larkspur as the guidelines in each bouquet (see Figure 19). Following the photograph, insert the spiky outline flowers, white and blue larkspur, red goldenrod, caspia, and blue statice, into that base. Add springerei next, turning the vase to check that the arrangement is well balanced. Lastly, brighten the color scheme with pink and white globe amaranth and white yarrow. Use the needle-nose pliers whenever necessary to add flowers to the arrangement without disturbing surrounding flowers.

5. Spray with clear matte fixative (see page 19).

Fig. 19. Outline of Painted Ladies

Oriental Tapestry

The colors in this oriental blue and orange export bowl served as the inspiration for the color scheme of this arrangement, with everyday flowers like marigolds taking on new importance in this kaleidoscope of color.

FLOWERS & FOLIAGE

Air-dried

statice (30 white)

larkspur (40 blue)

strawflowers (16 white, 30 orange)

globe amaranth (14 orange)

baby's breath (14)

Miscellaneous

sand-dried marigolds (20 orange)

springerei, stems (40 treated and dyed green)

Spanish moss

SIZE

Finished arrangement is 18″ wide × 18″ high.

MATERIALS

export bowl, 8″ in diameter

wood base (optional)

½ blocks floral foam

Davee or adhesive tape

thick white craft glue

clear matte spray fixative

knife

clippers

needle-nose pliers

INSTRUCTIONS

1. Read The Basics of Preserving and Arranging, pages 10–30.

2. Cut the floral foam to fit, allowing at least ½ inch to rise above the rim of the bowl and tape into place (see page 27). Cover with Spanish moss.

3. Following the photograph, outline the arrangement with springerei, blue larkspur, and white statice, turning the bowl as you work. Fill in with German statice. Being careful not to have two of the same type of flowers exactly opposite each other, place the marigolds, orange globe amaranth, and strawflowers. Add stems of baby's breath that have been dipped in glue last.

4. Spray with clear matte fixative (see page 19).

Five-Finger Posy Holder

A five-finger posy holder evokes memories of Williamsburg and its gracious Colonial style, which is enhanced by the red, white, and blue flowers that capture our country's spirit.

FLOWERS & FOLIAGE

Air-dried

larkspur (13 white, 12 blue)

statice (19 blue)

cockscomb (6 red)

roses (10 red)

baby's breath (20)

pearly everlasting (14 white)

Miscellaneous

sand-dried yarrow (10 white)

silica-gel-dried ranunculuses (7 white)

glycerinized goldenrod (8 dyed red)

pressed nandina leaves, stems (13)

SIZE

Finished arrangement is 19″ wide × 16″ high.

MATERIALS

five-finger posy holder

1 block floral foam

thick white craft glue

clear matte spray fixative

clippers

knife

needle-nose pliers

INSTRUCTIONS

1. Read The Basics of Preserving and Arranging, pages 10–30.

2. Fill the body of the vase with sand. Cut floral foam into 5 pieces measuring 2″ × 2″ × 2″. Place a block over each vase opening and push down to make a guide for cutting. Cut the plugs to fit the openings and place them to rise ¾″ above the rim of the "fingers" as shown in Figure 20.

Fig. 20. Outline of Five-Finger Posy Holder arrangement

44

3. The outline as shown in Figure 20 is made up of nandina leaves, filled in with white and blue larkspur, red goldenrod, and blue statice placed well back in the fingers of the vase. Working forward, continue adding these flowers along with cockscomb, pearly everlasting, and yarrow. Space the white ranunculuses as shown in the photograph. Glue the baby's breath in place last.

4. Spray with clear matte fixative (see page 19).

Autumn Beauty

This combination of yellow flowers with beige and brown leaves in a grapevine basket reflects the way we think of fall. The plants used here were picked in late summer and early fall, the flowers were sand-dried, and the leaves were preserved in glycerine. The only fragile flowers in this long-lasting arrangement are black-eyed Susans, which could be replaced with fresher ones next year. Using this creation of beige and brown as a backdrop, a flower in another color could change the look completely.

FLOWERS & FOLIAGE 🦎

Glycerinized

holly (3)

mountain laurel (7)

assorted leaves and branches (8)

mature hydrangeas (3 beige)

goldenrod (15 dyed yellow)

Miscellaneous

air-dried sweet Annie (artemisia), branches (10)

sand-dried black-eyed Susans (24)

SIZE

Finished arrangement is 21" wide × 24" high.

MATERIALS

grapevine vase, 4" in diameter × 8½" high

1 block floral foam

strip of floral clay

plastic mesh pot scrubber

clear matte spray fixative

knife

clippers

needle-nose pliers

INSTRUCTIONS

1. Read The Basics of Preserving and Arranging, pages 10–30.

2. Trim the floral foam to fit vertically into the basket at least 1 inch below the rim and rising 7 inches above it. Reinforce the foam with a plastic mesh pot scrubber or vegetable bag (see page 23). Place a strip of floral clay around the inside rim of the basket and insert the foam into it.

The leaves and flowers of the arrangement are so dense that no Spanish moss is necessary to conceal the foam.

3. Sweet Annie, a fragrant light brown form of artemisia, is used as outline material along with goldenrod and laurel branches. As shown in the photograph, these flowers are placed well back in the basket, and more are worked forward in the arrangement along with other glycerinized branches. Hydrangeas are placed, then black-eyed Susans are added last. Finish off the back of this one-sided arrangement with short pieces of goldenrod and branches.

4. Spray the black-eyed Susans with clear matte fixative (see page 19) before adding them, then spray the whole arrangement.

Flowers under a Dome

A dried floral arrangement, profuse with blossoms, placed under a glass dome creates a feeling of nostalgia for the last century. The Victorians placed all sorts of things under glass domes to protect them, including dried flowers. The glass dome calls attention to the flowers, then flatters them. An arrangement such as this should be displayed where it will be most appreciated.

FLOWERS & FOLIAGE

Air-dried

larkspur (12 pink)

strawflowers (10 pink, 10 white)

globe amaranth (10 pink)

pearly everlasting (15 white pieces, 10 dyed blue pieces)

baby's breath (28)

cockscomb (8 red pieces)

Sand-dried

nigella (10 white)

hydrangeas (12 blue pieces)

zinnias (8 pink)

Miscellaneous

silica-gel-dried roses (24 red, 14 pink, 12 maroon)

green sheet moss

SIZE

Finished arrangement is slightly smaller than the dome, 7½" wide × 11½" high.

MATERIALS

glass dome, 8" in diameter × 12" high

wooden base, 10" in diameter × ½" high

antique vase, 5" in diameter × 4" high

½ block floral foam

strip of floral clay

clear matte spray fixative

knife

clippers

needle-nose pliers

INSTRUCTIONS

1. Read The Basics of Preserving and Arranging, pages 10–30.

2. Shape the floral foam into a cone and place it either on top of or into the vase, which has been topped with a strip of floral clay. (See Figure 21.) Once the foam is secure, cover it with green sheet moss, holding it in place here and there with bent wires or small stems.

3. Place the vase in the middle of the wooden base. Using the rim of the base as a guide, arrange the round flowers, such as zinnias, roses, and strawflowers (rather than the usual spiky flowers), as the outline to come almost to the rim here and there all around. Measure the height of the dome and position the top flower accordingly, then place the dome over the flowers to check that they are about ½ inch away from the glass on all sides.

After the outline flowers are in place as shown in Figure 21, insert flowers such as hydrangeas deep into the arrangement to give it depth and to cover the floral foam. Fill in with spiky flowers

like larkspur and pearly everlasting, then with cockscomb, nigella, and globe amaranth to give a full, lush look. Add baby's breath here and there if a space needs to be filled. Needle-nose pliers will be necessary when working with flowers placed so closely together. Place the glass dome over the arrangement from time to time to make sure no flower is out of the outline.

4. To make doubly certain that humidity does not invade the dome, spray arrangement with clear matte fixative (see page 19), allow to dry thoroughly, and place under the dome.

5. Do not glue the dome to the base. If a few petals are dislodged when the arrangement is moved, you can remove them easily by carefully lifting the dome and blowing on the base.

Fig. 21. Outline of Flowers under a Dome

Formal Centerpiece

An ideal container for a centerpiece is a serving bowl that matches the china, as shown in the photograph. When using dried flowers the choice of vases and bowls is unlimited since there is no concern about water leaking on the table. Antique dishes with hairline cracks, or beautiful china pieces with missing tops or chipped edges take on new life as holders for dried flowers.

FLOWERS & FOLIAGE

Air-dried
statice (16 purple)

cockscomb (8 red)

sea lavender (36)

caspia (8 dyed rose)

larkspur (18 white)

salvia (20 blue)

nigella pods (10)

strawflowers (8 pink, 8 yellow)

echinops (12)

roses (12 red)

globe amaranth (14 orange, 14 white)

baby's breath (32)

Sand-dried
zinnias (12 pink)

hydrangeas (9 blue)

delphinium, individual blossoms (14 blue)

Silica-gel-dried
dahlias (6 yellow, 6 rust, 6 purple)

roses (20 pink, 10 off-white)

peonies (4 pink, 4 white)

Miscellaneous
pressed ferns, tips (10 sprayed green)

Spanish moss

SIZE
Finished arrangement is 22″ long × 14″ high.

MATERIALS
serving bowl, 10″ long × 8″ wide × 2½″ high

2 blocks floral foam

Davee or adhesive tape

floral tape

thick white craft glue

clear matte spray fixative

knife

clippers

needle-nose pliers

INSTRUCTIONS
1. Read The Basics of Preserving and Arranging, pages 10–30.

2. Trim the floral foam and tape it in place, rising at least ½ inch above the top of the bowl (see page 27).

3. Using Figure 15, on page 27, as a guide, place

the spiky sea lavender, caspia, and ferns as the outline of the arrangement. When the outline is established, fill in with more spiky air-dried flowers, such as purple statice, red cockscomb, white larkspur, blue salvia, nigella pods, and globe amaranth. Turn the container as you work edge of the container should bend over the sides in graceful curves.

When the arrangement thus far looks well balanced, add the larger air-dried flowers such as strawflowers and echinops, along with zinnias, hydrangeas, dahlias, roses, and peonies. Use the needle-nose pliers where necessary to keep from breaking the flowers. Use the photograph as a guide when adding these accent flowers. Finally, add the delphinium blossoms and baby's breath (their stems dipped in glue) here and there among the larger flowers.

4. Spray with clear matte fixative (see page 19).

Basket and Bow

This basket of flowers, although large, could be used as a centerpiece for a buffet table or be placed on a side table or on the floor. The colorful, dramatic bouquet in a basket is enhanced by a unique floral bow of pink larkspur.

FLOWERS & FOLIAGE

Air-dried

strawflowers (20 white, 20 pink)

globe amaranth (12 orange, 20 purple, 15 pink)

larkspur (20 pink, 20 blue, 20 white)

statice (32 purple)

curry plants (24 small bunches)

pearly everlasting (24 white, 10 dyed peach)

cockscomb (10 red, 10 pink)

sea lavender (32)

caspia (20 dyed pink)

poppy heads (15)
salvia (12 blue)

baby's breath (16)

rhodanthe (12 pink)

goldenrod (12 yellow)

yarrow (12 yellow)

Miscellaneous

sand-dried yarrow (8 white)

silica-gel-dried roses (16 pink)

glycerinized goldenrod (12 dyed red)

Spanish moss or green sheet moss

SIZE

Finished arrangement is 24" wide × 17" high.

MATERIALS

white basket, 11" at the widest part × 13" high (including the handle)

2 blocks floral foam

newspaper

Davee or adhesive tape

thick white craft glue

1 yd. upholstery trim or strong ribbon ½" wide

fabric stiffener or wallpaper paste

12" piece 20-gauge wire for bow

clear matte spray fixative

scissors

clippers

needle-nose pliers

INSTRUCTIONS

1. Read The Basics of Preserving and Arranging, pages 10–30.

2. Make the flower bow the day before the arrangement, allowing time for it to dry. Cut 1 yard of upholstery trim or strong ribbon ½ inch wide,

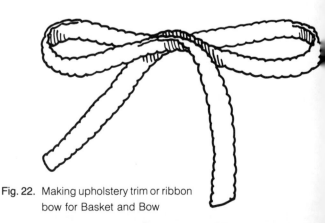

Fig. 22. Making upholstery trim or ribbon bow for Basket and Bow

54

dip it into a fabric stiffening agent or wallpaper paste, and shape it (do not tie it) in the form of a bow, as shown in Figure 22. Twist a wire around the middle to insert into the foam. Place the wired bow on waxed paper or foil to dry. Attach approximately 50 pink larkspur florets to the stiffened upholstery trim with thick craft glue. Allow the flowers to dry before adding the bow to the finished arrangement.

3. Crumple newspaper in the bottom of the basket and tape in place. Cut and trim floral foam to fit the basket, allowing it to rise at least ½ inch above the rim of the basket, and tape in place (see page 27). Cover foam with Spanish or green sheet moss.

4. Arrange the spiky flowers, pink, blue and white larkspur, blue salvia, sea lavender, pink caspia, and red goldenrod, for the outline following Figure 23. Add orange, purple, and pink globe amaranth; white and peach pearly everlasting; purple statice; and curry plant with slightly shorter stems than the outline material, staying within the guidelines. Turn the basket so the design is evenly balanced, but don't try to arrange one side of the basket and then match the other to it. Fill in with red goldenrod, red and pink cockscomb, poppy heads, pink rhodanthe, and white strawflowers. Then glue in baby's breath. Use needle-nose pliers to insert the final flowers.

5. Attach the bow by inserting its wire into the foam.

6. Spray arrangement, including bow, with clear matte fixative (see page 19).

Fig. 23. Outline for Basket and Bow

Apple Basket Ensemble

Dried flowers arranged in a cardboard apple basket covered with dried apple slices sounds more whimsical than beautiful, but the photograph says otherwise. Apples and roses are in the same botanical family and so harmonize well. Wreaths-of-flowers napkin rings and flower-bedecked candle holders made from whole apples complete this luxurious table setting.

FLOWERS & FOLIAGE

Air-dried
sweet Annie (artemisia), stems (24)

globe amaranth (15 white)

pearly everlasting (28 white)

strawflowers (20 off-white)

cockscomb (8 red)

roses (24 red)

money plants (10)

baby's breath (30)

Glycerinized
goldenrod (20 dyed red)

mountain laurel (16)

Miscellaneous
sand-dried yarrow (15 white)

silica-gel-dried roses (48 off-white)

pressed nandina leaves, stems (10)

Spanish moss

Basket Centerpiece

The colors of the flowers in this lush bouquet complement perfectly the apple slices decorating the container.

SIZE
Finished arrangement is 22″ long × 15″ high.

MATERIALS
cardboard apple basket, 10″ long × 6″ wide × 4″ high

treated dried apples, 60 slices (instructions follow)

2 blocks floral foam

thick white craft glue

clear matte spray fixative

scissors

clippers

knife

plastic knife for glue

needle-nose pliers

hot-glue gun and glue sticks

INSTRUCTIONS
1. Read The Basics of Preserving and Arranging, pages 10–30.

2. Dried apple slices can be purchased in craft shops and nurseries, or dried at home by slicing the apples, rubbing them with lemon juice, and drying them overnight in an oven on lowest heat.

The cardboard apple basket is one that holds apples purchased at a farm market. Fill the basket with floral foam rising ½ inch above the rim

57

and tape in place (see page 27). Attach the apple slices to the basket as shown in Figure 24 by applying hot glue to the basket and pushing the slices into it, overlapping as shown. When basket is completely covered, hide the floral foam with Spanish moss.

3. Outline the arrangement with spiky material such as sweet Annie, mountain laurel, nandina leaves, and red goldenrod. Fill in, using the photograph as a guide, with pearly everlasting, white yarrow, money plant, and strawflowers in varying lengths. Turn the basket as you add the

58

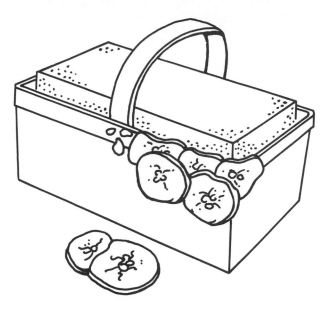

Fig. 24. Gluing treated apple slices to apple basket

flowers so the arrangement will be well balanced. Add the off-white and red roses to the bouquet using the needle-nose pliers to avoid crushing the flowers around them. Glue in baby's breath last.

4. Spray with clear matte fixative (see page 19).

Napkin Ring

This simple wreath adds an elegant touch to a table setting.

FLOWERS & FOLIAGE

Air-dried

pearly everlasting (4 white)

rose (1 red)

baby's breath (2)

SIZE

Finished napkin ring is 3¼″ in diameter.

MATERIALS

3″ wreath made of grapevine or similar stems

½ yd. red ribbon ¼″ wide

thick white craft glue

clear matte spray fixative

clippers

scissors

INSTRUCTIONS

1. Make a bow and glue it onto the wreath with thick craft glue.

2. Following the photograph, glue pearly everlasting, rose, and baby's breath to the wreath.

3. Allow time for the glue to dry, then spray with clear matte fixative (see page 19).

Candled Apple

The fresh apple used in this candle holder will soften and have to be discarded after a few days, but the candle pick and the wreath decorating it can be reused.

FLOWERS & FOLIAGE

Air-dried

pearly everlasting (10 white)

rose (1 red)

baby's breath (5)

berries (3 dyed red small bunches)

MATERIALS

apple

6" white candle

2" wreath made of grapevine or similar stems

½ yd. red ribbon ¼ " wide

candle pick

thick white craft glue

clear matte spray fixative

clippers

scissors

INSTRUCTIONS

1. Cut the stem out of the top of the apple and insert the candle pick, available in flower or craft shops, in that spot (see Figure 25).

2. Make a bow and glue it to the wreath.

3. Add the pearly everlasting, berries, rose, and baby's breath to the wreath with craft glue.

4. Allow the glue to dry, then spray with clear matte fixative (see page 19).

5. Place the wreath over the candle, hiding the base.

Fig. 25. Inserting candle pick into apple

60

Biedermeier Bouquets

Biedermeier, which originated in Vienna, Austria, is a classic design as well as a period in history. The style became popular in the 1900s and is recognized by compact circular arrangements of brilliantly colored lush blossoms. This form was popular for interior decoration, wreaths, and bridal bouquets. The Biedermeier style remains popular in Austria today.

FLOWERS & FOLIAGE

Air-dried
cockscomb (4 red pieces)

pearly everlasting (22 dyed rose pieces)

roses (15 red)

Silica-gel-dried
roses (22 off-white)

miniature roses (49 pink)

Miscellaneous
pressed ferns, tips (16 sprayed green)

Centerpiece

The large bouquet would complement any setting and is an ideal dinner table centerpiece for a special occasion. The small basket is a party favor.

SIZE
Finished centerpiece is 11" wide × 5" high.

Finished favor is 5" wide × 3" high.

MATERIALS
basket, 9" in diameter

2 blocks floral foam

Davee or adhesive tape

4 yds. deep red satin ribbon ⅝" wide

fine spool wire

clear matte spray fixative

knife

needle-nose pliers

INSTRUCTIONS
1. Read The Basics of Preserving and Arranging, pages 10–30.

2. Place a block of floral foam in the middle of the large basket. Cut the other block lengthwise and place half on either side. Trim to fit as shown in Figure 26, shaping the foam into a mound rising 3 inches in the center rather than the usual ½ inch. This allows the use of short stems to shape the rounded form of the finished bouquet. If it is necessary to elevate the floral foam, tape crumpled newspaper into the bottom of the basket and place the foam over it.

3. Break off the end pieces of the ferns and insert them around the basket as shown in Figure 26.

4. Starting just above the ferns, carefully add rows of flowers as shown in the photograph. Insert the stems, building upward, starting with off-white roses, then a circle of rose pearly everlasting, followed by a ring of deep-pink roses, then miniature pink roses, and lastly red cockscomb. Use needle-nose pliers where necessary to keep your hands out of the arrangement.

5. To make the side bows (see page 26), cut the ribbon in 1-yard lengths. Loop one end back and forth, hold one 12-inch streamer behind the loop, add another under that, and tie the bow and streamers together with a third streamer. Insert wire through the back of the knot, twist, and insert wire into floral foam near the base of the handle as shown in the photograph.

6. Spray with clear matte fixative (see page 19).

Fig. 26. Foam and ferns in Biedermeier centerpiece

FLOWERS & FOLIAGE

Air-dried
globe amaranth (15 white)
cockscomb (15 red pieces)

Silica-gel-dried
miniature roses (12 pink)
ranunculus (1 red)

Miscellaneous
sand-dried yarrow (8 white small pieces)
pressed rose leaves (11)

MATERIALS
basket, 3" in diameter
½ block floral foam
Davee or adhesive tape
2 yds. pink ribbon ¼" wide
fine spool wire
clear matte spray fixative
knife
needle-nose pliers

INSTRUCTIONS

1. The smaller basket is arranged in the same manner on a smaller scale.

2. Cut and trim floral foam to fit into basket with a center height of about 1 inch.

3. Place rose leaves around the outside edge just above the rim of the basket. If the stems are not long enough to insert into the foam, glue them in place.

4. Starting at the bottom, add a row of white globe amaranth just above the leaves, then a circle of short pieces of red cockscomb broken off a larger head. Follow with a row of pink roses, then white yarrow pieces broken off a large head, and top it all with a maroon ranunculus.

5. Make bows (see page 26) and attach them to basket handles.

6. Spray with clear matte fixative (see page 19).

Decorated Candlestick

Decorating candlesticks or candelabra with dried flowers is the easiest and quickest way to dress up a table or buffet. The hard green plastic flower holder, which fits into the candlestick, is called an O'dapter and is available in flower and craft shops.

For safety's sake, use a dripless candle and don't leave it burning when there's no one at the table.

FLOWERS & FOLIAGE

Air-dried

larkspur (12 pink)

pearly everlasting (20 white)

yarrow (10 white, broken up)

statice (12 purple)

strawflowers (8 pink)

globe amaranth (12 white, 12 pink)

hydrangeas (3 green, broken up)

curry plant (10 pieces)

German statice (16 pieces)

roses (6 red, 6 pink)

baby's breath (20)

Miscellaneous

silica-gel-dried roses (18 pink)

glycerinized goldenrod (14 dyed red pieces)

springerei (15 pieces treated and dyed green)

SIZE

Finished arrangement, without candlestick, is 16″ wide × 6″ high.

MATERIALS

candlestick

O'dapter

¼ block floral foam for insert

dripless candle

thick white craft glue

clear matte spray fixative

clippers

needle-nose pliers

INSTRUCTIONS

1. Read The Basics of Preserving and Arranging, pages 10–30.

2. Push the rubber tip of the O'dapter into the candlestick. Cut floral foam to fit, place floral foam insert into the holder (see Figure 27), and push candle into the foam. Do not make a hole—if regular Oasis is used the candle will press in easily.

Fig. 27. O'dapter with foam insert

3. Arrange springerei for the outline as shown in Figure 28, bending the stems over the edge of the green plastic holder to hide it and to give the arrangement a more graceful look. Follow similar lines with pink larkspur, pearly everlasting, purple statice, German statice, and red goldenrod.

Fill in the spaces with green hydrangeas, pink strawflowers, and yarrow. Keep turning the arrangement so that the sides are even. Check the symmetry of the arrangement before adding the roses and gluing in the baby's breath.

4. Spray with clear matte fixative (see page 19).

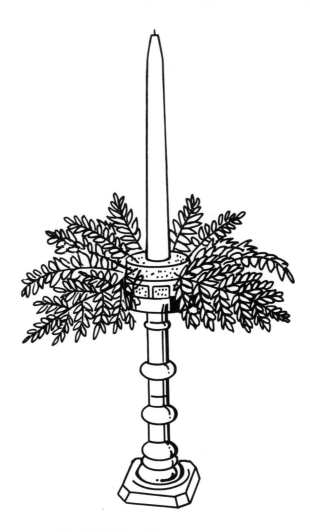

Fig. 28. Outline of Decorated Candlestick

WEDDING FLOWERS

The key to a successful wedding is planning—the farther ahead the plans are made, the better. Using dried wedding flowers allows the bride time to choose her flowers and color scheme with care. Because it isn't always possible to visualize every facet of the wedding flowers in advance, drying the bouquets gives the bride time to ask for corrections if any are needed.

Store the flowers in a warm, dry room, along with, perhaps, the bride's dress.

Dried flowers should not be used outdoors unless they have had at least two coats of clear matte protective spray and the humidity is very low. Anything else is a gamble.

The floral arrangements in this chapter were made to complement the color scheme of one wedding, but you can substitute flowers in the colors of your choice.

See pages 28-30 for details about using dried flowers for a wedding.

Bridal Bouquet

This wedding bouquet represents beauty at its best. It shows not only the splendor of the flowers but celebrates the skill in preserving and arranging the blossoms. Any bride would be thrilled to carry this bouquet on her wedding day and, if it's handled with care, to enjoy it for a long time afterward.

Dried flowers are fragile and need special treatment. It is a good idea to have someone place the bouquet in a weighted bud vase at the wedding party's table after the ceremony.

FLOWERS & FOLIAGE

Sand-dried

nigella (6 white)

yarrow (9 white)

dogwood, blossoms (5 white)

Silica-gel-dried

ranunculuses (4 white)

hyacinth, individual blossoms (15 white)

roses (5 off-white)

lilies of the valley (10)

peonies (3 white)

Miscellaneous

air-dried larkspur (11 white)

pressed ferns, tips (12 sprayed green)

SIZE

Finished bouquet is 12″ wide × 15″ high.

MATERIALS

bouquet holder, 3¾″ in diameter

off-white lace collar for bouquet holder

white floral tape

2 yds. off-white satin ribbon ½″ wide

3 yds. off-white lace ribbon 1¼″ wide

fine spool wire

clear matte spray fixative

scissors

needle-nose pliers

INSTRUCTIONS

1. Read The Basics of Preserving and Arranging, pages 10–30.

2. Wrap the handle of the bouquet holder with white floral tape. Then wrap satin ribbon around the taped handle.

3. To establish the bouquet's guidelines, outline the edges with ferns, then larkspur.

4. After the larkspur is in place, make a double bow with streamers (see page 26), attach wire through the back of the knot, and insert the wire into the floral foam of the holder.

5. Working from the outside, fill in with the sand-dried flowers and then the silica-gel-dried flowers as shown in the photograph, leaving the peonies until last. The peonies and perhaps some other flowers will have to be carefully placed using needle-nose pliers.

When working with lily of the valley, tape three stems together with white floral tape and insert them as one for greater visual impact.

6. Spray with two light coats of clear matte fixative (see page 19) and store in a warm, dry room.

Bride's Hat

A flower-bedecked wedding hat is very romantic, combining the splendor of beautiful flowers with the taste and personality of the bride.

FLOWERS & FOLIAGE

Air-dried
strawflowers (2 white)

larkspur (4 white)

Sand-dried
dogwood, blossoms (2 white)

yarrow (2 white)

roses (6 off-white)

Silica-gel-dried
ranunculuses (4 white)

peony (1 white)

lilies of the valley (6)

Miscellaneous
assorted pressed ferns, tips (10 sprayed green)

SIZE
Finished hat is 18″ in diameter, with a 5″ crown.

MATERIALS
straw hat, 18″ in diameter

4 yds. off-white lace ribbon 1¼″ wide

2 yds. ivory satin ribbon ⅝″ wide

2 yds. off-white lace ribbon 5″ wide

clear matte spray fixative

scissors

hot-glue gun and glue sticks

needle-nose pliers

INSTRUCTIONS

1. Read The Basics of Preserving and Arranging, pages 10–30.

2. Secure a band of 1¼-inch lace around the hat with hot glue. Cut 11 pieces of lace and satin ribbons 20 to 21 inches long and glue them to the base of the crown. Glue the peony to the crown of the hat directly over the ribbons. Make two bows with short streamers (see page 26) and glue them to the crown on either side of the peony.

3. Glue the ferns in place here and there, leaving the tips free. Arrange the flowers on either side of the peony, with the larkspur along the band, facing toward the front.

4. Give the flowers two light coats of clear matte spray fixative (see page 19) and store in a warm, dry room.

Maid of Honor's Bouquet

The maid of honor's bouquet is a colorful reflection of the bride's flowers. Varying shades of pink with blue and white make this a striking expression of the wedding color scheme.

FLOWERS & FOLIAGE

Air-dried

hydrangeas (4 green, broken up)

larkspur (8 pink)

baby's breath (9)

Sand-dried

nigella (5 blue)

larkspur (8 pink, 5 blue)

yarrow (9 white)

Silica-gel-dried

lilies of the valley (7)

roses (12 pink, 5 off-white)

peonies (3 pink)

Miscellaneous

pressed ferns, tips (12 sprayed green)

SIZE

Finished bouquet is 12" wide × 15" high.

MATERIALS

bouquet holder, 3¾" in diameter

off-white lace collar for bouquet holder

white floral tape

2 yds. white satin ribbon ½" wide

4 yds. off-white lace ribbon ⅝" wide

fine spool wire

thick white craft glue

clear matte spray fixative

scissors

needle-nose pliers

INSTRUCTIONS

1. Read The Basics of Preserving and Arranging, pages 10–30.

2. This bouquet is assembled the same way as the bridal bouquet, pages 68–69. Wrap the holder handle in tape and then, with tape holding the ribbon in place, in satin ribbon.

3. Place the ferns first, adding short stems of green hydrangeas as a base for the flowers. Use pink larkspur for the outline of the bouquet, then add the blue larkspur. Make a double bow (see page 26), attach wire through the back of the knot, and insert it into the center of the bouquet holder before adding the rest of the flowers. Work from the outside in. Add the flowers carefully, using the needle-nose pliers when necessary.

Tape three stems of lily of the valley together with floral tape and insert them as one.

Add the peonies just before gluing the baby's breath.

4. Spray with two light coats of clear matte fixative (see page 19) and store in a warm, dry room.

Junior Bridesmaid's Basket

The pink basket filled with green, white, and pink flowers is an appropriate bouquet for a young girl to carry down the aisle.

FLOWERS & FOLIAGE

Air-dried

hydrangeas (10 green pieces)

larkspur (17 white, 18 pink)

strawflowers (5 pink)

pearly everlasting (10 dyed rose)

statice (10 white)

globe amaranth (12 pink)

baby's breath (16)

Miscellaneous

sand-dried larkspur (18 pink)

silica-gel-dried miniature roses (14 pink)

Spanish moss

SIZE

Finished bouquet is 12″ long × 9″ high.

MATERIALS

basket, 6″ long × 3″ wide × 3″ high, sprayed pink

1 block floral foam

Davee or adhesive tape

8 yds. pink satin ribbon ¼″ wide

white floral tape

thick white craft glue

fine wire

clear matte spray fixative

scissors

needle-nose pliers

INSTRUCTIONS

1. Read The Basics of Preserving and Arranging, pages 10–30.

2. Fill the basket with floral foam, allowing at least ½ inch to rise above the rim. Conceal the foam with a light covering of Spanish moss.

3. Wrap the handle with pink ribbon as shown in the photograph and tie ends securely.

4. Cover the foam with green hydrangea in 3-inch stems. If the stems are too short, extend them with wire and floral tape as described on page 21. Arrange the white larkspur to form the guidelines for the arrangement, next add the pink air-dried larkspur, filling in with the other flowers as shown in the photograph. Add pink sand-dried larkspur and rose pearly everlasting as shown in the photograph. Insert roses, strawflowers, and globe amaranth as shown in the photograph, turning the basket as you work. Glue pieces of baby's breath in place last.

5. Make two ribbon bows (see page 26). Slip a wire behind the knot and insert into the foam near the handle.

6. Spray the arrangement with two light coats of clear matte fixative (see page 19) and store in a warm, dry room.

Bridesmaids' Bouquets

These delicate and colorful nosegays echo the colors in the maid of honor's bouquet and are suitable for both formal and informal weddings.

FLOWERS & FOLIAGE
Pink Bouquet

Air-dried
> hydrangeas (5 green pieces, wired if necessary)
>
> larkspur (13 pink)
>
> globe amaranth (5 pink)
>
> strawflowers (5 pink)
>
> baby's breath (12)

Silica-gel-dried
> roses (5 off-white, 9 pink)
>
> peony (1 pink)

Miscellaneous
> sand-dried larkspur (12 pink)
>
> pressed ferns, tips (12 sprayed green)

Blue Bouquet

Air-dried
> hydrangeas (5 green, broken up)
>
> strawflowers (3 white)
>
> larkspur (3 blue)
>
> baby's breath (12)

Sand-dried
> nigella (6 blue)
>
> delphinium, individual blossoms (6 light blue, 6 dark blue)
>
> hydrangea (1 blue)

Miscellaneous
> silica-gel-dried roses (12 off-white)
>
> pressed ferns, tips (12 sprayed green)

SIZE
Each finished bouquet is 8″ wide × 5″ high.

MATERIALS (for each bouquet)
> bouquet holder, 3¾″ in diameter
> off-white lace collar for bouquet holder
> white floral tape
> 4 yds. off-white lace ribbon ⅝″ wide
> thick white craft glue
> clear matte spray fixative
> scissors
> needle-nose pliers

INSTRUCTIONS
1. Read The Basics of Preserving and Arranging, pages 10–30.

2. Before constructing the bouquet, wrap the holder's plastic handle first in white floral tape, then, with tape holding the ribbon in place, in off-white lace ribbon. Make a lace bow and streamers (see page 26). Use a streamer to tie the bow to the handle at the base of the bouquet. You could also use a chenille (pipe cleaner) to attach the bow.

3. Pink Bouquet: Cover the floral foam with hydrangea pieces, gluing them in place if necessary. Position the peony in the center of the floral foam so that it rises 5 inches above the lace. Place the other flowers around the peony, balancing color, texture, and size, using the needle-nose pliers where necessary. Add the delicate roses, then dip the ends of the baby's breath stems in glue and place here and there as accents.

Blue Bouquet: First insert the ferns at the edges of the bouquet. Then cover the foam with small pieces of green hydrangea, some of which will remain visible. Using the photograph as a guide, insert the larkspur and strawflowers. Carefully place the blue hydrangea in the center of the bouquet, then fill in with the nigella and delphinium. Finish up with the roses, then glue in the baby's breath.

Use the needle-nose pliers whenever necessary to place flowers without damaging surrounding ones.

4. Spray with two light coats of clear matte fixative (see page 19) and store in a warm, dry room.

Flower Girl's Ensemble

Basket

A very young flower girl often has trouble carrying even a lightweight basket comfortably because the size, as well as the weight, makes it awkward for her. The graceful solution seems to be in this small, lightweight wall basket dressed up with flowers and paper ribbon. As she walks it can hug her side, still looking like a flower-filled basket but without being heavy or clumsy.

FLOWERS & FOLIAGE

Air-dried

rosebuds (6 pink)

larkspur, blossoms (9 blue, 9 white)

strawflowers (3 pink)

baby's breath (9)

Miscellaneous

Oasis Moss Mate (9" × 2")

SIZE

Finished arrangement is 9½" long × 9" high.

MATERIALS

wall basket, 7½" at the widest part × 9" high (including handle)

2 yds. rose paper ribbon 8" wide

thick white craft glue

clear matte spray fixative

hot-glue gun and glue sticks

scissors

INSTRUCTIONS

1. Read The Basics of Preserving and Arranging, pages 10–30.

2. After untwisting the 8-inch-wide paper ribbon (see page 25), measure a strip 10 inches long. Smooth it across the front of the wall basket horizontally, then fold it over the back on all four sides as shown in Figure 29. The paper can be

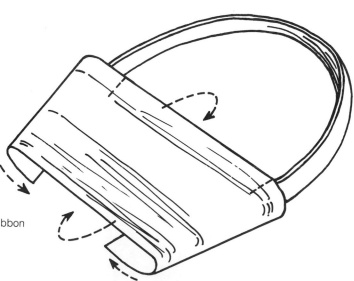

Fig. 29. Covering wall basket with paper ribbon

attached with either hot glue or craft glue. Craft glue takes longer to dry. Cut remaining ribbon into strips ¾ inch wide and use part to wrap the handle, gluing at each end. With the rest make the bow and streamers (see page 26).

3. Cut a strip of Oasis Moss Mate 9 inches × 2 inches. Glue it across the top in the space to be occupied by the flowers, bringing it over the edge toward the back.

4. Using the basket as a pattern, cut a piece of paper ribbon; glue it to the back of the basket to give a finished look.

5. Attach the bow and streamers with hot glue.

6. Arrange the larkspur, strawflowers, and then rosebuds around the bow. Use hot glue for the larger flowers and craft glue for the smaller. Finish by gluing baby's breath. Glue a strawflower to the center of the bow.

7. Spray two light coats of clear matte fixative (see page 19) and store in a warm, dry room.

Hat

This little straw hat is banded in the same rose-colored paper ribbon used to cover the flower girl's basket and to make the hanging basket (page 85) and curved arch (page 87). The addition of flowers in the bridal colors ties together the dainty ensemble.

FLOWERS & FOLIAGE

Air-dried

larkspur (5 pink, 5 blue, 5 white)

strawflowers (3 pink)

baby's breath (6)

Miscellaneous

pressed ferns, tips (7 pieces sprayed green)

SIZE

The hat is 12″ in diameter, with a 3½″ crown.

MATERIALS

2 yds. rose paper ribbon 8″ wide

thick white craft glue

clear matte spray fixative

scissors

hot-glue gun and glue stick

INSTRUCTIONS

1. Read The Basics of Preserving and Arranging, pages 10–30.

2. Untwist the paper ribbon (see page 25) and cut a strip 1 inch wide and long enough to go around the hat. Cut the remaining untwisted paper into 2½-inch widths and form into a bow and streamers (see page 25). Glue the band around the hat and the bow to the band using the hot-glue gun.

3. Use craft glue to attach the ferns, and hot glue for the larkspur and strawflowers. Baby's breath should be held in place with craft glue. Place some flowers under the bow loops and glue a pretty grouping on top of the bow.

4. Give the flowers two light coats of clear matte spray fixative (see page 19) and store in a warm, dry room.

Radiant Pedestal Display

The floral design used for this pedestal arrangement for the church or hall is of the radiating type. The flowers for this grand bouquet were arranged in a florist's papier-mâché container wrapped in white net.

FLOWERS & FOLIAGE

Air-dried

artemisia, stems (60)

larkspur (25 white)

pearly everlasting (30 white)

baby's breath (16)

Miscellaneous

silica-gel-dried peonies (16 white)

glycerinized eucalyptus (24)

Spanish moss

SIZE

Finished arrangement is 35" wide × 25" high.

MATERIALS

papier-mâché container, 6" in diameter × 6" high

3 yds. white net ribbon 6" wide

1½ blocks floral foam

Davee or adhesive tape

thick white craft glue

clear matte spray fixative

scissors

clippers

knife

hot-glue gun and glue sticks (optional)

INSTRUCTIONS

1. Read The Basics of Preserving and Arranging, pages 10–30.

2. Wrap the netting around and around the papier-mâché container until you have achieved the softening effect you desire, then secure with hot glue or craft glue.

3. Trim each corner of the whole block of floral foam so that it fits snugly into the container vertically, rising about 2 inches above the top. Cut the half block in two lengthwise and place the pieces on either side of the whole block so the foam fits securely. Tape the foam in place.

4. Following the photograph, place the eucalyptus first and the white larkspur next, establishing the outline for the arrangement. Fill in with artemisia and white yarrow. Peonies and baby's breath (with stems dipped in craft glue) are added last.

5. Spray with clear matte fixative (see page 19) and store in a warm, dry room.

Hanging Basket

An undistinguished basket is dressed up for the wedding and then filled with lovely flowers that pick up the bridal colors, giving this floral decoration a sense of occasion.

FLOWERS & FOLIAGE

Air-dried

German statice (20)

pearly everlasting (12 dyed rose)

larkspur (10 blue, 10 white)

larkspur, buds (8 blue, 8 white)

Miscellaneous

bear grass, stems (12 treated and dyed green)

Spanish moss

SIZE

Finished basket is 11″ wide × 11″ high.

MATERIALS

basket, 6″ in diameter × 11″ high (including handle)

3 yds. rose paper ribbon 8″ wide

1½ yds. white paper ribbon 4″ wide

1 block floral foam

white chenille (pipe cleaner)

clear matte spray fixative

clippers

scissors

hot-glue gun and glue sticks

INSTRUCTIONS

1. Read The Basics of Preserving and Arranging, pages 10–30.

2. Cut three pieces of untwisted rose paper ribbon 15 inches long. Follow the directions on page 25 to cover the container. Cut a 1-yard strip, untwist, and smooth. Cut into 1-inch strips lengthwise. Wrap the handle with 1-inch strips until it is completely covered and hot-glue each end. Finish by wrapping a 1-inch strip around the rim of the basket. Make two small bows with streamers (see page 25) and glue in place.

3. Fill the basket with floral foam cut to fit, rising ½ inch over the rim. Cover with moss.

4. Arrange the flowers in a radiating manner as in Figure 15 on page 27. Use pearly everlasting as the outline. Fill in with the other flowers, making sure that they curve over the edge.

5. Spray with clear matte fixative (see page 19).

6. Make a 24-inch white paper bow with 20-inch streamers (see page 25) and attach with a white chenille.

Paper Ribbon Arch

This oversized paper ribbon bow and small bouquet could decorate the top of a doorway or arch, the edge of the bridal party's table, or, as shown in the photograph, an antique wicker chair.

FLOWERS & FOLIAGE ✺❧

Air-dried

larkspur (9 pink, 8 blue)

strawflowers (9 pink)

globe amaranth (8 white, 8 pink)

baby's breath (9)

Fig. 30. Wrist corsage holder with floral foam

SIZE

Ribbon arch is 44″ long.

MATERIALS

wrist corsage holder

3 yds. rose paper ribbon 8″ wide

floral foam, 2″ × 2″ square × 1″ thick

fine spool wire

clear matte spray fixative

scissors

hot-glue gun and glue sticks

wire cutters (needle-nose pliers)

INSTRUCTIONS

1. Read The Basics of Preserving and Arranging, pages 10–30.

2. Untwist the paper ribbon (see page 25). Read the directions for making a paper ribbon bow, page 25. The bow on the arch has an additional loop.

The loop for the bottom bow measures 34 inches and the top loop measures 30 inches. Fold the untwisted ribbon under itself and place the top loop (with ends folded under) directly over that. Center a 50-inch piece around the loops and tie it around the middle. Puff up the loops and trim and notch the ends.

3. If your wrist corsage holder has metal prongs, push the piece of floral foam onto them securely. If there are no prongs, hot-glue the foam onto the center of the holder (see Figure 30). The holders are available in craft or flower shops.

4. Following the photograph, insert flowers into the foam. First place larkspur and strawflowers, then fill in with globe amaranth. Keep colors and shapes balanced. Glue in baby's breath last.

5. Spray with clear matte fixative (see page 19).

6. Loop wire through the knot in back of the bow and attach it to a nail on the mantel or door frame. If possible use hot glue to hold the arch in place. Wires tied around the ribbon just up from the notch hold the streamers in place, allowing it to form a curve as shown above.

Wedding Table Centerpiece

A basket centerpiece of the bridal colors in a light and airy arrangement sets the scene for the gaiety and celebration of the wedding day.

FLOWERS & FOLIAGE

Air-dried

German statice (1 large bunch, broken up)

caspia (1 small bunch, broken up)

larkspur (30 white, 30 pink, 30 blue)

Miscellaneous

bear grass, stems (20 treated and dyed green)

springerei, stems (20 treated and dyed green)

Spanish moss

SIZE

Finished arrangement is 24″ long × 15″ high.

MATERIALS

basket, 11″ long × 8″ wide × 4″ deep

2 blocks floral foam

4 yds. rose paper ribbon 8″ wide

Davee or adhesive tape

clear matte spray fixative

scissors

clippers

hot-glue gun & glue sticks

INSTRUCTIONS

1. Read The Basics of Preserving and Arranging, pages 10–30.

2. Trim and secure floral foam with tape, allowing at least ½ inch to rise above the rim (see page 27). Cover lightly with Spanish moss.

3. Untwist paper ribbon (see page 25) and cut 1 yard in half lengthwise. Use this strip to wrap the handle. Make two bows (see page 25) and glue it in place with a glue gun.

4. The flowers in the basket radiate from the center. Place the central pink larkspur, then the rest of the pinks as shown in the photograph. The white larkspur are added next, then the blue. Intersperse the flowers with greens, and place short stems of caspia and German statice deep into the arrangement.

5. Spray the finished arrangement with two light coats of clear matte fixative (see page 19) and store in a warm, dry room.

Guest Table Centerpieces

This charming basket is more than beautiful; it holds delightful little mementos for the guests. It mimics the wedding table centerpiece in color and use of flowers; only the style of arrangement is different. The edge of the basket is covered with Moss Mate, then decorated with flowers. The flower "arrangement" consists of three colors of larkspur peeking out of net bags filled with candied almonds, which serve as favors.

FLOWERS & FOLIAGE

Air-dried

larkspur, individual florets (68 white, 68 blue, 68 pink)

larkspur, short stems (8 white, 8 blue, 8 pink)

German statice (68 short pieces)

Miscellaneous

springerei, short stems (4 treated and dyed green)

Oasis Moss Mate (1 yd. × ½ yd.)

SIZE

Finished basket is 12″ long × 7″ deep (excluding handle); basket contains 8 net bags of almonds.

MATERIALS

basket, 10″ long × 6″ wide × 4″ deep (excluding handle)

3 yds. rose paper ribbon 8″ wide

4 yds. white netting 6″ wide

thick white craft glue

clear matte spray fixative

white thread

scissors

hot-glue gun and glue sticks (optional)

sewing machine or needle

candied almonds

INSTRUCTIONS

1. Read The Basics of Preserving and Arranging, pages 10–30.

2. Oasis Moss Mate is a plastic sheet with short pieces of green moss glued to it, and is available in craft or flower shops. Cut a strip of Moss Mate 4 inches wide and as long as necessary and glue it around the edge of the basket, allowing 2 inches both inside and outside the basket.

3. Cut a 1-yard length of untwisted paper ribbon (see page 25) in half lengthwise and wrap the handle, hot-gluing it in place at each end. Make two bows (see page 25) and hot-glue in place on both sides of the basket.

4. Apply hot glue to the moss and push individual larkspur florets into it rather than risk burns by trying to put the glue on the flowers. Distribute the three colors evenly. Add the German statice and the greens.

5. Spray the basket flowers with two light coats of clear matte fixative (see page 19). Spray the larkspur that will decorate the net bags before arranging them, to avoid possibly spraying the candy.

6. To make the net bags, cut pieces of netting 4 inches by 6 inches. Finished bags are 2 inches wide and 3 inches high. Fold netting in half and stitch the bottom and one side, then add the almonds.

7. Place one larkspur stem of each color inside the bag. Tie the bag closed with a bow made of paper ribbon cut to a width of 1 inch.

8. Place the bags in the basket with the flowers pointed upward, framed by a ring of flowers.

Wedding Cake Decorations

This elegant cake is encircled and topped by lush multicolored flowers.

FLOWERS & FOLIAGE

Air-dried

hydrangeas (8 green, broken up)

larkspur (18 pink, 18 blue)

pearly everlasting (42 white, 26 dyed pink)

strawflowers (28 pink)

globe amaranth (50 white, 30 pink)

baby's breath (42)

Sand-dried

hydrangeas (6 blue, broken up)

zinnias (8 deep pink)

delphinium, individual blossoms (12 blue)

Miscellaneous

silica-gel-dried roses (18 pink, 24 off-white)

springerei, long stems (8 treated and dyed green, broken up)

Spanish moss

Cake Wreath

The cake was placed on a three-inch pedestal so it would rise above the flowers. Ribbon was wrapped around each five-inch layer of cake to improve the balance in relation to the wreath.

SIZE

The finished wreath is 25″ wide × 5″ high.

MATERIALS

20″ wire wreath frame

5 blocks floral foam

nylon filament (fishing line)

3 yds. rose grosgrain ribbon ½″ wide

clear matte spray fixative

knife

clippers

scissors

INSTRUCTIONS

1. Read The Basics of Preserving and Arranging, pages 10–30.

2. Read the instructions for making a wire wreath frame, pages 21–22. Cut the floral foam in half, measure, cut, and fill wire base. Cover with Spanish moss and tie with nylon filament.

3. There is no particular order in which you should decorate the wreath, but a good start is to distribute the green hydrangea pieces all around. Following the photograph, add the air-dried flowers. Insert the more delicate sand-dried and silica-gel-dried flowers, then fill in with springerei. Finish by gluing in stems of baby's breath.

Be sure to keep the flowers, colors, and shapes

balanced throughout the wreath. Check often as you work to make sure you have enough of any flower left to go all around the wreath.

4. Spray wreath with two light coats of clear matte fixative (see page 19) and allow to dry thor-oughly before placing around cake. If possible, have someone help lower the wreath over the cake.

This luxurious wreath can also be hung by its wire base.

Cake Top

The bouquet of flowers on top of the cake should be in proportion to the cake itself and to the other flowers used. The cake was not ornately decorated, allowing the flowers to take center stage.

FLOWERS & FOLIAGE

Air-dried

strawflowers (5 off-white, 5 pink)

pearly everlasting (3 white, 8 dyed pink)

lavender (9)

baby's breath (12)

Miscellaneous

sand-dried larkspur (9 blue, 5 pink)

silica-gel-dried roses (6 pink, 6 off-white)

springerei, stem (1 treated and dyed green, broken up)

SIZE

Finished arrangement is 4″ wide × 3″ high.

MATERIALS

Junior Miss bouquet holder, 2½″ in diameter

thick white craft glue

clear matte spray fixative

scissors

needle-nose pliers

INSTRUCTIONS

1. Read The Basics of Preserving and Arranging, pages 10–30.

2. Either break off the handle of the bouquet holder or wrap it in foil so it can be pushed into the cake.

3. Following the photograph, create a radiating arrangement. Insert the lavender as the outline. Add the strawflowers and pearly everlasting, then distribute the larkspur and roses. Fill in with pieces of springerei and glue in short stems of baby's breath. Balance the flowers, colors, and shapes.

4. Spray arrangement with two light coats of clear matte fixative (see page 19) and allow to dry thoroughly before placing on cake.

5. After placing the holder on the cake, encircle the base with ribbon as a finishing touch.

WREATHS

Wreaths have become a symbol of welcome when hung outside the house, and of cheerfulness and beauty when displayed indoors. The wreaths shown in this book are for indoor use, to protect the dried flowers from humidity.

Wreaths are made on frames of straw, wire, grapevine, and wicker, all of which are available in craft shops, nurseries, and flower shops.

The perfect seasonal decoration, a wreath would be a striking gift for any occasion, and particularly appropriate to welcome friends to their new home.

Patchwork Wreath

This design is a marvelous way to use up your floral leftovers. Many times there are small amounts of a variety of flowers that would be lost in an arrangement, but look their best in this design.

FLOWERS & FOLIAGE

Air-dried

curry plant (9 pieces)

strawflowers (7 white)

globe amaranth (16 pink)

rhodanthe (10 pink)

pearly everlasting (10 dyed peach, 10 dyed rose)

cluster-flowered everlasting (13 yellow)

nigella pods (7)

statice (16 purple small pieces)

globe amaranth (16 purple)

goldenrod (12 dyed red)

cockscomb (6 red)

strawflowers (7 rust)

baby's breath (12 small bunches)

Sand-dried

delphinium, individual blossoms (7 light blue, 7 dark blue)

nigella (11 white)

hydrangeas (7 blue pieces)

Miscellaneous

silica-gel-dried roses (6 off-white)

Spanish moss

SIZE

Finished wreath is 12″ in diameter.

MATERIALS

10″ wire wreath frame

1 block floral foam

nylon filament (fishing line)

thick white craft glue

clear matte spray fixative

knife

clippers

needle-nose pliers

INSTRUCTIONS

1. Read The Basics of Preserving and Arranging, pages 10–30.

2. Follow the general directions for preparing a wire wreath frame, pages 21–22.

3. Begin by laying out the flowers in a rough design or by sketching the design on paper. Place light colors next to dark ones for greater impact. Because the colors of dried flowers are muted there is less risk of color clashes, which makes combining colors easier. It is impossible, as you see in the photograph, to try to make flowers conform to an exact space, since they come in all shapes and sizes.

4. The flowers are pushed into the prepared wreath vertically so they can be seen to their best advantage. (See Figure 7 on page 22.) Each stem can be dipped into the thick glue before inserting into the wreath if desired.

5. Spray the finished wreath with clear matte fixative (see page 19).

Heart of Flowers

A heart-shaped wire frame was used for this dainty wreath in red and white. It communicates a message of love by its form and the beauty of the flowers.

FLOWERS & FOLIAGE

Air-dried

roses (45 red)

baby's breath (1 bunch)

Miscellaneous

glycerinized goldenrod (12 dyed red)

Spanish moss

SIZE

Finished wreath is 12″ at the widest part.

MATERIALS

heart-shaped wire wreath, 10″ wide (at the widest part)

1 block floral foam

nylon filament (fishing line)

thick white craft glue

clear matte spray fixative

knife

clippers

needle-nose pliers

INSTRUCTIONS

1. Read The Basics of Preserving and Arranging, pages 10–30.

2. Follow the general directions for preparing a wire wreath frame, pages 21–22.

3. Break off stems of goldenrod and insert into wreath all along the inside and outside edge. Arrange red roses as shown in photograph and fill in with short stems of baby's breath. If necessary dip the stems in glue before placing them in the frame.

4. Spray the completed wreath with clear matte fixative (see page 19).

Golden Circle

This combination of yellow and gold dried flowers set into a wire frame makes a glorious welcome-to-autumn wreath.

FLOWERS & FOLIAGE

Air-dried

strawflowers (24 pale yellow)

baby's breath (40)

yarrow (40 yellow small pieces)

cluster-flowered everlasting (10 white)

feverfew (12)

Miscellaneous

sand-dried black-eyed Susans (30)

glycerinized goldenrod (34 dyed yellow)

bloom broom (15 small bunches dyed yellow)

Spanish moss

SIZE

Finished wreath is 12″ in diameter.

MATERIALS

10″ wire wreath frame

1 block floral foam

nylon filament (fishing line)

thick white craft glue

clear matte spray fixative

knife

clippers

needle-nose pliers

INSTRUCTIONS

1. Read The Basics of Preserving and Arranging, pages 10–30.

2. Follow the general directions for preparing a wire wreath frame, pages 21–22.

3. Following the photograph, insert the flowers vertically into the wreath, showing them to their best advantage (see Figure 7 on page 22). Each stem can be dipped in glue before being placed in the wreath. Start with the strawflowers, yarrow, feverfew, and cluster-flowered everlasting, then add the goldenrod and bloom broom. Goldenrod needs to be broken up into smaller stems. Add black-eyed Susans and baby's breath last.

4. Spray the finished wreath with clear matte fixative (page 19).

Dainty Blue Wreath

This wreath of blue flowers has only a touch of baby's breath to serve as a contrast to the "blues." It is not only lovely but has the added advantage of being quickly and easily made on a wire wreath frame.

FLOWERS & FOLIAGE

Air-dried

German statice (1 small bunch)

baby's breath (1 small bunch)

Sand-dried

larkspur (80 blue)

delphinium, individual blossoms (30 light blue, 30 dark blue)

Miscellaneous

Spanish moss

SIZE

Finished wreath is 12″ in diameter.

MATERIALS

10″ wire wreath frame

1 block floral foam

nylon filament (fishing line)

pole pins (optional)

thick white craft glue

clear matte spray fixative

knife

clippers

needle-nose pliers

INSTRUCTIONS

1. Read The Basics of Preserving and Arranging, pages 10–30.

2. Follow the general directions for preparing a wire wreath frame, pages 21–22.

3. Insert the flowers vertically into the wreath frame to show them off to the best advantage (see Figure 7 on page 22). If the flowers are heavy, dip them into glue first. Begin with the German statice, then add the larkspur. Finish by placing the individual delphinium blossoms and gluing the baby's breath.

4. Spray the finished wreath with clear matte fixative (see page 19).

Biedermeier Wreath

The Biedermeier wreath, inspired by that Victorian period in Austria, elicits the same feelings of excitement as the Biedermeier baskets on page 62. A wire wreath frame was chosen for this design because the flowers can be inserted straight into the wreath, allowing the full impact of the open flowers.

FLOWERS & FOLIAGE

Air-dried

curry plants (12)

roses (13 red)

pearly everlasting (24 white, 13 dyed pink)

baby's breath (16)

Sand-dried

zinnias (13 maroon)

hydrangeas (6 blue)

Miscellaneous

silica-gel-dried roses (16 pink, 12 red)

glycerinized goldenrod (4 dyed red)

Spanish moss

SIZE

Finished wreath is 12" in diameter.

MATERIALS

10" wire wreath frame

1 block floral foam

nylon filament (fishing line)

thick white craft glue

clear matte spray fixative

knife

clippers

needle-nose pliers

INSTRUCTIONS

1. Read The Basics of Preserving and Arranging, pages 10–30.

2. See the general directions for preparing a wire wreath frame, pages 21–22.

3. Start the design from the inside and work out. Place red goldenrod on the inside of the wreath, pushing the stems into the foam. To keep them flattened so they do not fill in the center, glue the stems down with craft glue or hold them in place with pole pins. The next row is made up of pearly everlasting, with silica-gel-dried red roses interspersed in its midst. This is followed by blue hydrangeas with pink roses. The outer rim is made up of maroon zinnias, accented with yellow curry plants and air-dried red roses. Glue short pieces of baby's breath into the wreath as shown in the photograph. If flowers are especially large or heavy, the stems should be dipped into glue before inserting them into the wreath frame.

4. Spray the finished wreath with clear matte fixative (see page 19).

Decorated Straw Wreath

The flowers for the base of this elegant straw wreath are attached with pole pins. The larger flowers on wire stems are dipped in glue and inserted directly into the straw. Other flowers are glued onto the base to add a special color or texture.

FLOWERS & FOLIAGE

Air-dried

hydrangeas (6 green, broken up)

German statice (1 small bunch)

nigella pods (18)

cockscomb (15 red pieces)

baby's breath (1 small bunch)

Sand-dried

yarrow (10 white, halved)

roses (9 maroon)

zinnias (8 dark red)

Miscellaneous

silica-gel-dried roses (14 red)

glycerinized goldenrod (12 dyed red)

SIZE

Finished wreath is 14" in diameter.

MATERIALS

12" straw wreath

pole pins, 1" long

12" piece of 20-gauge wire

thick white craft glue

clear matte spray fixative

clippers

needle-nose pliers

INSTRUCTIONS

1. Read The Basics of Preserving and Arranging, pages 10–30.

2. Remove the green wrapping from the frame. Follow the directions on page 22 to make a wire hanger.

3. Assemble dried flowers and pole pins. Start by making small bunches of German statice, hydrangeas, nigella pods, and cockscomb (see Figures 16A and 16B on page 28) and attaching them to the outside of the wreath with the pole pins as shown in Figure 31. Work across the wreath to the inside, placing the next row so that the top of each bunch is just covering the pin of the previous row. Do not place flowers farther up than that or when the wreath is finished it will be chunky looking instead of full. Continue in rows, always just covering the previous row's pins, until the wreath is covered. Add flowers to

Fig. 31. Attaching flowers to a straw wreath with pole pins

form the design you have in mind or use the photograph as a guide.

4. Open roses or other delicate flowers should be glued in place after the other flowers have been attached. Glue baby's breath in last. Allow an hour or so for the glue to dry before hanging the wreath.

5. Spray with clear matte fixative (see page 19).

Ribbons and Flowers

An innovative idea and an easy way to tie in colors is to wrap a straw wreath with paper ribbon, cap that with a ribbon-bedecked bow, and add flowers for excitement. Other ribbons may be used but the beauty of paper ribbon is its ability to hold its shape and stay fresh looking indefinitely. This wreath can, of course, be replicated in any number of color combinations.

FLOWERS & FOLIAGE

Air-dried

pearly everlasting (12 small bunches white)

strawflowers (12 light pink, 12 dark pink)

globe amaranth (20 pink)

cockscomb (10 pieces pink)

springerei, long stems (2 treated and dyed green, broken up)

Sand-dried

larkspur (10 pink, broken up)

roses (12 pink)

nigella (10 white, 10 blue)

SIZE

Finished wreath is 14" in diameter.

MATERIALS

12" straw wreath

8 yds. pink paper ribbon 4" wide

3 yds. floral ribbon 1¼" wide

12" piece of 20-gauge wire

thick white craft glue

clear matte spray fixative

scissors

clippers

hot-glue gun and glue sticks

INSTRUCTIONS

1. Read The Basics of Preserving and Arranging, pages 10–30.

2. Untwist paper ribbon (see page 25) and wrap completely around a straw wreath from which the green plastic has been removed. Cut one piece 20 inches long for the bow, and three other pieces the same length for streamers. Glue the floral ribbon down the middle of each piece with craft glue and set aside to dry. After the glue has dried, make a bow as shown on page 25. Hot-glue the two streamers to the place earmarked for the bow, then glue the bow over the streamers. Puff up the bow and the ties, gluing so that the puffs stay in place. Remember to put the glue onto the wreath and not on the bow to lessen the chances of burning yourself. Once the bow and streamers are in place, notch the ends.

3. Start by gluing the air-dried flowers to the ribbon on the bottom half of the wreath. Distribute the cockscomb, strawflowers, and globe amaranth, then fill in with the smaller flowers. Balance the flowers, colors, and shapes.

4. Spray with clear matte fixative (see page 19).

HOLIDAYS

Flowers are a necessary holiday decoration, and when dried flowers are used to make these festive arrangements they can be kept and used the following year as well. In addition, they can be prepared well in advance, which is a great help since holidays are such a busy time. Dried flower decorations can begin at the front door and continue throughout the house.

Sometimes the flowers and plants themselves represent the holiday or season. Red roses tell us it's Valentine's Day. Daffodils and pussy willows speak of spring. Orange marigolds, pumpkins, gourds, corn, and colored leaves symbolize the fall holidays of Halloween and Thanksgiving. Evergreens, pine cones, and red berries evoke Christmas.

Have fun with colorful ribbons (e.g., plaid or velvet for Christmas) and accessories (such as glitter, pearls, dolls, and birds) on your holiday decorations. And having the whole family help decorate increases everyone's enjoyment of the occasion.

Glorious Christmas Decorations

The coordinated garland, nosegay, and mirror swag will brighten your home for the long Christmas season.

FLOWERS & FOLIAGE

Air-dried

cockscomb (18 red pieces)

German statice (1 small bunch)

strawflowers (8 white, 8 pink)

hydrangeas (10 green pieces)

baby's breath (12)

Silica-gel-dried

peonies (4 pink)

roses (6 red)

Miscellaneous

sand-dried zinnias (8 deep pink)

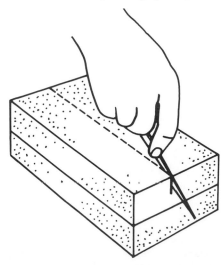

Fig. 32. Cutting floral foam for Christmas Garland

Garland

A green garland embellished with dried flowers is a festive Christmas decoration that can be used on a staircase or a mantel with equal success.

SIZE

One loop in the flower garland is 38" long.

MATERIALS (for one 38" loop)

artificial evergreen garland, approximately 40" long

4 plastic bags 6" wide × 10" high

1 block floral foam

12 twist ties or chenilles (pipe cleaners)

20-gauge wire

thick white craft glue

clear matte spray fixative

knife

clippers

needle-nose pliers

hot-glue gun and glue sticks

INSTRUCTIONS

1. Read The Basics of Preserving and Arranging, pages 10–30.

2. Attach the artificial evergreen garland to the bannister with chenilles (pipe cleaners), twist ties, or 20-gauge wire.

3. Cut floral foam into quarters as shown in Figure 32.

4. Slip one quarter piece of foam into each of the four plastic bags, leaving enough plastic on each end to attach it to the next bag, as shown in Fig-

ure 33. Use twist ties to hold the foam in the bag and to attach the four bags to one another.

5. Place the plastic-bag garland on a worktable and insert flowers into the floral foam by pushing stems through the plastic. If flowers are especially large or heavy, dip the stems into craft glue first. For flowers without stems, use hot glue.

Decorate each plastic-bag-and-foam section of the garland as follows. Place a peony, or other large specimen flower, in the center, and a zinnia, or other large flower, at each end. Then add strawflowers and the other flowers in descending size order. Fill in with German statice and the little flowers, and glue in baby's breath last.

6. Spray with clear matte fixative (see page 19).

7. Use chenilles or 20-gauge wire to attach the flower garland to the artificial garland. Any wire flowers stems that protrude from the back of the flower garland can also be used.

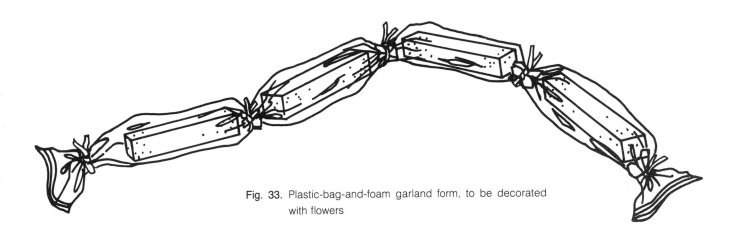

Fig. 33. Plastic-bag-and-foam garland form, to be decorated with flowers

Nosegay

Dried flower nosegays are attached to the garland between loops, to add an even more festive touch. Nosegays can also be attached to chairs, curtains, archways, and so forth, or be displayed in weighted vases.

FLOWERS & FOLIAGE

Air-dried

cockscomb (4 deep pink pieces)

globe amaranth (5 pink)

strawflowers (3 pink)

German statice (6)

pearly everlasting (8 white)

baby's breath (10)

Sand-dried

larkspur (6 pink)

zinnias (3 pink)

Miscellaneous

silica-gel-dried roses (7 pale pink, 6 red, 3 maroon)

pressed ferns, tips (10 sprayed green)

springerei, stems (5)

SIZE

Finished nosegay is 7″ in diameter and 3″ high.

MATERIALS (for one nosegay)

Junior Miss bouquet holder, 2½″ in diameter

lace or paper collar for bouquet holder

floral tape

4 yds. red satin ribbon ¼″ wide

4 yds. pink satin ribbon ¼″ wide

thick white craft glue

clear matte spray fixative

chenille (pipe cleaner) or twist tie

clippers

scissors

needle-nose pliers

INSTRUCTIONS

1. Read The Basics of Preserving and Arranging, pages 10–30.

2. Before starting the bouquet, wrap the holder handle with floral tape. Then, with tape holding the ribbon in place, wrap with satin ribbon. Make pink and red satin bows according to the directions on page 26 and attach now or when the bouquet is finished. Either tie the bow on with one of its streamers or insert a short chenille (pipe cleaner) through the bow's knot and attach with that.

3. Place pieces of fern around the outer edge of the holder just inside the lace collar. Insert a maroon rose in the center and three pink zinnias around it. Place pink globe amaranth, cockscomb, roses, and strawflowers around the zinnias and between them and the center rose. This bouquet should look as if it is brimming with flowers, but leave some spaces in between the flowers for short stems of German statice, springerei, and baby's breath. Continue toward the outer edge with these flowers, ending with pink larkspur and pearly everlasting near the edge of the ferns. Use needle-nose pliers as necessary when inserting flowers.

4. Spray with clear matte fixative (see page 19).

5. Attach the nosegay to the garland with a chenille (pipe cleaner) or a twist tie.

Festooned Mirror

The garland-topped mirror echoes the colors and materials used in the adjoining garland on the stairway and is made the same way. If your mirror would look top-heavy with the thickness of two garlands, the flower stems can be dipped into craft glue and attached directly to the artificial garland.

FLOWERS & FOLIAGE

Air-dried

cockscomb (18 red pieces)

German statice (1 small bunch)

strawflowers (8 white, 8 pink)

hydrangeas (10 green pieces)

baby's breath (12)

Silica-gel-dried

peonies (4 pink)

Miscellaneous

sand-dried zinnias (8 deep pink)

SIZE

Finished flower garland is 36″ long.

MATERIALS

artificial evergreen garland, approximately 38″ long

4 plastic bags 6″ wide × 10″ high

floral foam

13 twist ties or chenilles (pipe cleaners)

20-gauge wire

thick white craft glue

clear matte spray fixative

knife

clippers

needle-nose pliers

hot-glue gun and glue sticks

INSTRUCTIONS

1. Read The Basics of Preserving and Arranging, pages 10–30.

2. Attach the artificial garland to the mirror with chenilles, twist ties, or 20-gauge wire.

3. Follow steps 3 through 7 for the Garland, pages 111–113.

New Year Champagne Tree

A Christmas tree in a champagne bucket bridges the season and extends the time of holiday cheer. The tree is an artificial one, so if care is used it may be stored with the decorations intact and used more than one year.

FLOWERS & FOLIAGE

Air-dried

strawflowers (16 pink)

cockscomb (12 red pieces)

globe amaranth (12 white, 12 pink)

nigella pods (12)

baby's breath (24)

goldenrod (12 dyed red)

larkspur (15 pink)

Sand-dried

larkspur (15 pink)

zinnias (12 deep pink)

Silica-gel-dried

peonies (3 white)

roses (12 red, 12 pink, 12 white)

Miscellaneous

Spanish moss

SIZE

Finished tree is 15″ wide × 32″ high.

MATERIALS

artificial evergreen tree, 24″ high

champagne bucket

container for liner, 5″ in diameter × 5″ high

plaster of Paris

thick white craft glue

clear matte spray fixative

clippers

INSTRUCTIONS

1. Read The Basics of Preserving and Arranging, pages 10–30.

2. Most artificial trees are sold with the branches hugging the trunk. Pull the branches down and toward the front, leaving the back flat so it may be placed against the wall.

3. Prepare the plaster of Paris according to the directions, mixing it in the 5-inch container. A papier-mâché vase or anything that holds water can be used. Push the base of the trunk into the plaster and hold in place until it sets up. Decorate when the plaster is thoroughly dry.

4. Place the tree in its container in the champagne bucket. Cover the plaster with moss.

5. Dip each flower stem into craft glue and insert it into the tree. Using the photograph as a guide, start with the air-dried flowers: larkspur, strawflowers, cockscomb, globe amaranth, nigella pods, and goldenrod. Try to balance the colors and shapes throughout. Add the sand-dried larkspur and zinnias, then the roses. Insert the peonies just before gluing in the baby's breath.

6. Allow the glue to dry thoroughly before moving the tree and before spraying it with clear matte fixative (see page 19).

Valentine's Day Heart

Because this luxurious romantic arrangement needed a solid support, a Styrofoam base was used. There was no danger of it splitting, as Styrofoam so often does, since the base is 2 inches thick and the dried flowers are lightweight. Flower stems (natural or wire) are inserted into the Styrofoam. Other flowers are glued in place.

FLOWERS & FOLIAGE

Air-dried
strawflowers (8 white, 8 pink)

cockscomb (15 red pieces, 12 pink pieces)

larkspur (5 white, 5 pink)

globe amaranth (12 white, 12 pink)

baby's breath (10 pieces)

Sand-dried
zinnias (8 pink, 5 maroon)

lily of the valley (12)

Silica-gel-dried
roses (14 off-white, 20 pink, 16 red)

hyacinth, florets (10 white)

ranunculuses (10 pink, 10 maroon, 6 white)

Miscellaneous
green sheet moss

SIZE
Finished arrangement is 14" at the widest part.

MATERIALS
solid Styrofoam heart, 11" in diameter

thick white craft glue

clear matte spray fixative

clippers

needle-nose pliers

hot-glue gun and glue sticks

INSTRUCTIONS

1. Read The Basics of Preserving and Arranging, pages 10–30.

2. Cover the heart with green sheet moss and glue it here and there. You can use either craft glue or hot glue. Don't cover the heart completely with glue, as it dries hard and makes it more difficult to insert the stems. The flowers will help to hold the moss in place.

3. Start in the center and radiate from there using different shades of red and pink. Some flowers, such as cockscomb, can be broken up into smaller flowers and glued into place, while others, like roses, can be pushed into the base on their natural or wire stems. It is usually easier to decorate the top of the wreath and then the sides. Small flowers may have to be inserted between large ones using needle-nose pliers.

Easter's Reflection

The spring flowers pictured here are not normally found in a dried flower arrangement, which makes them all the more appealing. They look so fresh, it's necessary to point out to admirers that they are indeed dried. This combination of flowers would also be lovely in a basket. The cork container was chosen because it has a "woodsy" appearance, which complements the unsophisticated look of the flowers.

FLOWERS & FOLIAGE

Sand-dried
dogwood, branches (6)
lily of the valley (10)

Miscellaneous
air-dried pussy willows (12)
silica-gel-dried daffodils (9)
pressed ferns (8 sprayed green)
bun moss

SIZE
Finished arrangement is 24″ long × 14″ high.

MATERIALS
cork or other container, 7″ in diameter
1½ blocks floral foam
Davee or adhesive tape
bun moss
fine spool wire
floral tape
clear matte spray fixative
clippers
knife
needle-nose pliers

INSTRUCTIONS
1. Read The Basics of Preserving and Arranging, pages 10–30.

2. Cut floral foam to fit, leaving ½ inch above the rim of the container, and tape if necessary (see

Fig. 34. Arranging Easter's Reflection

page 27). Cover foam with bun moss, held in place with "hairpins" made of fine wire.

3. Following Figure 34 and the photograph, carefully insert the curved pussy willow branches that outline the arrangement into the floral foam and moss. The pussy willow was coaxed into this shape by curving it inside a bucket while it was fresh and pliable and allowing it to dry in the air for a week or ten days. The ferns are arranged in an unstudied design reflecting the woodsy look of the arrangement. If the stems on the ferns are not long enough, extend them with wire (see page 21). Add the daffodils and lily of the valley. Dogwood branches come last to balance the asymmetry of the pussy willows.

4. Spray with clear matte fixative (see page 19).

Harvest Pride

This dramatic centerpiece accompanied by tiny pumpkins and corncob dolls belongs on a Thanksgiving or harvest table. The visual and emotional impact is great but the expense is small. Miniature pumpkins and ornamental corn are found in farm markets and nurseries. The large pumpkin can be a real one or made of ceramic. The possibilities for this type of decoration are endless.

FLOWERS & FOLIAGE

Air-dried

sweet Annie (artemisia) (12)

teasel (12 natural, 12 bleached)

pearly everlasting (24 white, 24 dyed peach)

strawflowers (10 rust, 16 yellow)

wheat, stems (12)

feverfew, stems (10)

blackberry lilies (20)

Sand-dried

marigolds (16 orange, 16 yellow)

yarrow (20 white)

zinnias (14 yellow)

Miscellaneous

ginkgo leaf roses (instructions follow, page 126)

glycerinized goldenrod (24 dyed yellow)

Spanish moss

Pumpkin Centerpiece

A pumpkin bouquet of yellow and orange flowers and stems of wheat is the perfect decoration for a harvest feast.

SIZE

Finished centerpiece is 20″ wide × 20″ high.

MATERIALS

pumpkin, 9″ in diameter × 8″ high

container, 4″ in diameter × 6″ high (optional liner)

1 block floral foam

plastic mesh pot scrubber

newspaper

clear matte spray fixative

clippers

needle-nose pliers

INSTRUCTIONS

1. Read The Basics of Preserving and Arranging, pages 10–30.

2. If a fresh pumpkin is to be used, hollow it out, leaving an opening 4 inches in diameter. The arrangement can be made using the pumpkin as a container, but a more practical approach is to construct the arrangement in a liner that can be lifted out and used again when the pumpkin becomes too soft. A coffee can measuring 4 inches in diameter × 6 inches high is a good liner.

3. Reinforce the foam by covering it with a plastic mesh pot scrubber (see page 23).

4. Stuff crumpled newspaper in the bottom of the liner or pumpkin to raise the foam 4 inches above the rim of the pumpkin when inserted vertically. Insert the foam. It should fit snugly.

5. Using the photograph as a guide, insert a combination of goldenrod and teasel to produce a rounded outline so the arrangement can be made to reflect the form of the pumpkin. The floral foam rising above the rim of the pumpkin allows the tall, straight stems to be inserted

downward at a graceful angle to maintain the shape.

6. Turn the pumpkin often as the bouquet is created to keep it well balanced. After placing the goldenrod and teasel, add the other sturdy air-dried material until the arrangement has taken

125

shape. If you have some marigolds or zinnias that are less than perfect, push them deep into the arrangement for added interest. Then add the accent flowers such as marigolds, zinnias, yarrow, strawflowers, and blackberry lilies, as shown in the photograph. The blackberry lily seeds resemble a blackberry, and make a natural contrast to the rest of the flowers. The gingko leaf roses are added last. Use the needle-nose pliers whenever necessary when inserting flowers to avoid damaging surrounding flowers.

7. Spray with clear matte fixative (see page 19).

Gingko Leaf Roses

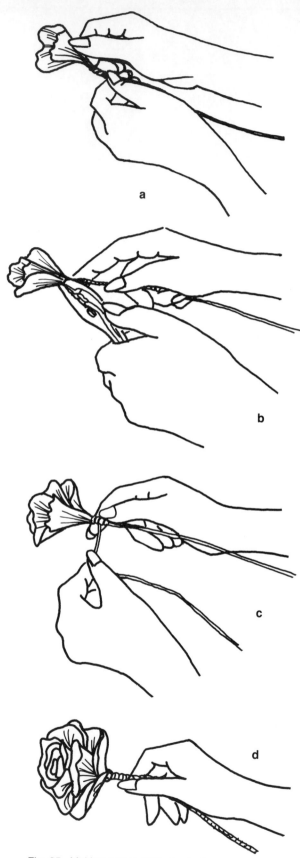

A contrived rose made of gingko leaves turns a beautiful medium brown when it dries, giving added interest to a fall arrangement. The gingko leaf is especially successful because it is so sturdy, but if it is not available experiment with other leaves, including ones that have been glycerinized. The finished roses can also be sand- or silica-gel-dried rather than air-dried as these were.

SIZE

Finished rose is approximately 2″ in diameter.

MATERIALS

15 gingko leaves (approximately) for each rose

fine spool wire

floral tape

20-gauge wire

needle-nose pliers

INSTRUCTIONS

1. Fold over the leaf as shown in Figure 35A, then roll it tightly around the end of a 20-gauge wire to serve as a stem, fastening it with fine wire. Needle-nose pliers hold the leaf securely while wrapping it (Figure 35B).

2. Continue wrapping the leaves progressively more loosely around the first, securing them with fine wire (Figure 35C).

3. Wrap and wire leaves until the desired size is achieved (Figure 35D). Put aside in a warm, dry place to dry in the air.

Fig. 35. Making a rose from gingko leaves

Corncob Doll

A corncob doll makes an enchanting party favor or decoration to add to the harvest or Thanksgiving table, especially when combined with pumpkins, large and small. This doll uses miniature ears of corn, but larger dolls can be made with regular-size ornamental corn.

SIZE

Finished doll is 10″ tall.

MATERIALS (for 1 doll)

3 ears miniature ornamental corn

1¼″ Styrofoam ball

scissors

hot-glue gun and glue sticks

INSTRUCTIONS

1. Ornamental corn, already dried, is available at farm markets and supermarkets in the fall. When the corn was freshly picked the husks were peeled back above the cobs. Three or four ears were tied together and hung so both the husks and the ears could dry. If you grow your own corn, do the same, and then hang them over a clothesline in a warm, dry place.

Carefully remove the husks from one ear of corn, but not from the other two.

2. Soak all the husks in warm water until they are pliable. In order to keep the cobs that are still attached to husks dry, place all the husks in a large jar filled with warm water with the ears extending up and out of the water.

3. Remove husks from the water and place two cobs side by side for the legs, with their husks flat on the table above them. Place the third cob crosswise on top of the husks for the arms.

4. Bend the husks down over the cob, forming a tunic and skirt. Tie one strip of husk around the waist of the doll (see Figure 36) to secure.

5. Cover the Styrofoam ball with the loose third husk, tying a strip below and above the ball to hold the husk in place. The pieces below the tie will be the collar, and the pieces above, the hair. Trim and fringe the ends as needed.

6. When the corn husk is completely dry, attach the head to the body with hot glue.

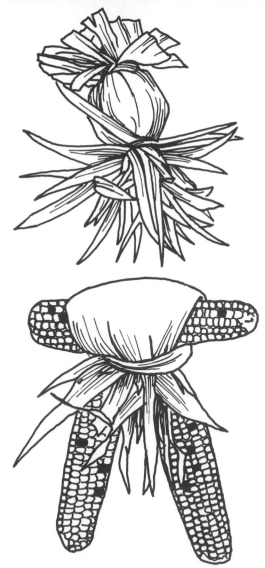

Fig. 36. Making a corncob doll

Decorated
Miniature Pumpkins

Miniature pumpkins are so pretty and delicate, and when they are embellished with dried flowers, they become attractive place card holders and charming party favors.

SIZE

Largest finished arrangement is approximately 3" in diameter.

MATERIALS (for 1 pumpkin)

miniature pumpkin

3 or 4 strawflowers, hemlock cones, or other small dried flowers, including baby's breath

raffia or narrow ribbon

clear matte spray fixative (optional)

scissors

hot-glue gun and glue sticks

INSTRUCTIONS

1. Make a bow of ribbon or raffia.

2. Experiment placing the bow and the dried flowers around the top of the pumpkin stem. When the arrangement looks pleasing and balanced, attach the bow and the flowers to the pumpkin with hot glue.

3. Because these materials are so sturdy, spraying with clear matte fixative (see page 19) is not necessary. If you would prefer the extra protection, however, spraying never hurts the flowers.

GIFTS

A present of dried flowers in any one of their beautiful forms is always welcome. There is no more charming way to say "thank you" or "I love you" than with flowers, and if a special token has been fashioned with the lucky recipient's favorites, the giftgiver is truly speaking the language of flowers.

Dried flowers are so versatile that they can be made into a wide assortment of gifts for every occasion. Some of the gifts shown here take some time to make; others take just moments. Even the simplest are lovely, and will be delights to receive.

Pretty Yellow Basket

This basket, whether it's filled with soap, candy, or love letters, would add a cheerful note to any room. It is a perfect gift for any occasion.

FLOWERS & FOLIAGE

Air-dried

curry plants (15 small bunches)

strawflowers (14 yellow, 14 white)

globe amaranth (16 white)

Miscellaneous

sand-dried marigolds (2 yellow)

bloom broom (30 dyed yellow small bunches)

Oasis Moss Mate 23" long × 3½" wide

SIZE

Finished arrangement is 10" long × 8½" wide.

MATERIALS

yellow basket, 7" long × 4" wide × 3½" deep

1 yd. yellow paper ribbon 4" wide

thick white craft glue

clear matte spray fixative

scissors

clippers

plastic knife for glue

hot-glue gun and glue sticks

INSTRUCTIONS

1. Read The Basics of Preserving and Arranging, pages 10–30.

2. Glue the strip of Oasis Moss Mate around the edge of the basket with craft glue, allowing 1½ inches inside and 1½ inches outside.

3. Untwist 1 yard of yellow paper ribbon (see page 25) and cut into 1-inch strips. Make a bow with long streamers (see page 25) and attach it to the handle with hot glue. Wrap the streamers around the handle and glue here and there to hold the loops in place. Glue the marigolds over the ends of the paper ribbon on the sides of the basket.

4. Following the photograph, hot-glue the yellow and white strawflowers to the moss. Attach the smaller flowers, such as curry plant, globe amaranth, and bloom broom, with craft glue.

5. Spray with clear matte fixative (see page 19).

Flower Combs

Flower combs are a lovely gift that will please every young lady. Use tiny flowers of your choice. These were made to coordinate with the bouquets in the wedding chapter.

FLOWERS & FOLIAGE

Pink Combs

Air-dried

larkspur, blossoms (6 pink, 4 white)

baby's breath, short stems (6)

Miscellaneous

pressed ferns, tips (4 sprayed green)

Pink and Blue Combs

Air-dried

larkspur, blossoms (6 white, 6 blue)

baby's breath, short stems (6)

Silica-gel-dried

roses (4 pink)

nigella, blossoms (2 blue)

Miscellaneous

pressed ferns, tips (4 sprayed green)

MATERIALS

pair of good-quality combs

thick white craft glue

clear matte spray fixative

scissors

plastic knife for glue

INSTRUCTIONS

1. Read The Basics of Preserving and Arranging, pages 10–30.

2. Spread glue thickly across the top of each comb.

3. Glue a fern end to each side of each comb, leaving the tip free to extend beyond the comb. Following the photograph, carefully place each floret.

4. Spray with clear matte fixative (see page 19) and allow combs to dry overnight before wearing.

Baby Gifts

Pink, pretty, and sweetly sentimental describes this gift for the new mother of a baby girl. She'll enjoy looking at it, and if the tops are saved and tucked into a little bag, the bottles can be used when the arrangement has lost its luster. Alternative flowers are listed for a blue gift for a boy. Or you could create your own arrangement with flowers of any colors.

FLOWERS & FOLIAGE
Pink Arrangement

Air-dried

> pussy willow (5)
> heather (5 rose)
> larkspur (9 pink)
> baby's breath (12)

Silica-gel-dried

> roses (5 pink)
> miniature roses (20 pink)

Blue Arrangement

Air-dried

> pussy willow (5)
> larkspur (8 blue, 6 white)
> baby's breath (12)

Miscellaneous

> sand-dried delphinium, individual blossoms
> (10 blue, 10 white)

SIZE

Finished arrangement with bottles side by side is 9½" long × 19" high.

MATERIALS

> 1 pink baby's milk bottle (or blue or white)
> 1 pink baby's juice bottle (or blue or white)
> sand
> ½ block floral foam
> clear matte spray fixative
> clippers
> needle-nose pliers

INSTRUCTIONS

1. Read The Basics of Preserving and Arranging, pages 10–30.

2. Fill the bottles with sand up to 2 inches from the rim. Cut a plug of floral foam for each bottle opening that fits 2 inches below the rim and rises ½ inch above it.

3. Following the photograph, outline the twin arrangement as one, using pussy willow and heather as the guidelines. Add pink larkspur and the larger pink roses. Because they will show, reinforce the wire stems of the roses with dried stems and wrap with floral tape.

The fine wires of the miniature roses are inserted into the foam above the rim, to hide the foam and to give added interest to the arrangement. Glue baby's breath last.

4. For the blue arrangement, use pussy willow and larkspur to make the outline. Fill in with larkspur, then insert delphinium blossoms into the foam around the rim of the bottle. Glue baby's breath here and there in the arrangement.

5. Spray flowers with clear matte fixative (see page 19).

134

Cup, Saucer, and Flowers

Arranging flowers to echo the colors and design on the container doubles the pleasure. This would make a charming gift for a collector of china cups and saucers. (See the photograph on page 142.)

FLOWERS & FOLIAGE

Air-dried

larkspur (3 white)

baby's breath (8)

ferns (10 sprayed green)

Miscellaneous

sand-dried nigella (5 blue, 5 white)

silica-gel-dried roses (3 small maroon, 1 large maroon)

green sheet moss

SIZE

Finished arrangement is 6″ in diameter × 8″ high.

MATERIALS

cup and saucer

½ block floral foam

clear matte spray fixative

knife

INSTRUCTIONS

1. Read The Basics of Preserving and Arranging, pages 10–30.

2. Cut floral foam to fit into the cup snugly, then cover it with dried green sheet moss.

3. Following the photograph on page 142, outline the arrangement in white larkspur and ferns. Arrange the specimen flowers, in this case the maroon roses, to best advantage, and surround them with blue and white nigella to fill in the arrangement. Add baby's breath last.

4. Cover cup and saucer to protect them and spray with clear matte fixative (see page 19).

Lacy Lingerie Fragrancers

These lacy potpourri holders are too pretty to hide in a drawer—their loveliness should be seen at least part of the time. (See the photograph on page 142.)

Linen Sachet

A linen cocktail napkin takes on new life when filled with potpourri and tucked into a drawer.

SIZE
Finished sachet is 6" long × 3½" wide.

MATERIALS
potpourri, 1 cup
cocktail napkin, 12" long × 7" wide
½ yd. satin ribbon ¼" wide
needle and thread
scissors

INSTRUCTIONS
1. Follow the general directions for making potpourri, page 148.

2. Fold the napkin in half. Stitching on the hemline of the lace, sew three sides, leaving an opening for the potpourri.

3. Fill with potpourri and stitch up the opening.

4. Make a ribbon bow (see page 26) and tack it to the center of one edge of the napkin.

Tubular Sachet

The open ends of this lace-covered tube permit the fragrance to circulate, filling the air with the scent of flowers.

SIZE
Finished sachet is 9½" long × 2" wide.

MATERIALS
potpourri, 1 cup
1 cardboard tube 4½" long × 1¾" in diameter
lace 12" long × 10½" wide
2 yds. ribbon ½" wide
scissors

INSTRUCTIONS
1. Follow the general directions for making potpourri, page 148.

2. Wrap the tube in lace and tie a bow at one end.

3. Fill the open end with potpourri and tie a bow on that end.

Moss and Potpourri Basket

Moss and potpourri make a fragrant and attractive combination, and a perfect gift for yourself or others. (See the photograph on page 142.)

FLOWERS & FOLIAGE

sand-dried zinnias (2 dark red)

silica-gel-dried roses (3 pale pink, 2 pink, 1 off-white, 1 maroon)

petals (5 cups)

potpourri (4 cups)

green sheet moss (20" long × 4" wide for basket, 14" long × 1" wide for handle)

Fig. 37. Gluing sheet moss to Moss and Potpourri Basket

SIZE

Finished arrangement is 9" in diameter × 12" high.

MATERIALS

basket, 9" diameter × 12" high (including handle)

thick white craft glue

4 yds. maroon ribbon ⅝" wide

scissors

plastic knife for glue

INSTRUCTIONS

1. Read The Basics of Preserving and Arranging, pages 10–30.

2. Follow the general directions for making potpourri, page 148.

3. Glue the 14-by-1-inch piece of green sheet moss to the basket handle. Glue the 20-by-4-inch piece of green sheet moss to the outside rim of the basket with at least 1 inch on the inside, as shown in Figure 37. Patch where necessary.

4. Spread glue on the outside of the basket and press petals into the glue. Broken petals are fine.

5. Crisscross the ribbon around the handle and tie a bow at each end.

6. Fill the basket with potpourri and place specimen flowers on top for accent.

Peekaboo Petals

Recycled clear stationery boxes show the potpourri, and when opened bring the fragrance of summer into the room. This is preservation at its best. You can also use any box with a clear cover. (See the photograph on page 142.)

FLOWERS & FOLIAGE

Yellow Box

Sand-dried

marigold and zinnia petals made into potpourri (1½ cups)

pansies (5 yellow)

Blue Box

Sand-dried

larkspur, delphinium, and hydrangea petals made into potpourri (1½ cups)

larkspur, florets (10 dark blue)

delphinium, floret (1 light blue)

SIZE

Each box is 7" long × 5" wide.

MATERIALS

2 clear plastic boxes, 7" long × 5" wide

1½ yds. blue satin ribbon ⅝" wide

1½ yds. gold satin ribbon ⅝" wide

thick white craft glue

scissors

INSTRUCTIONS

1. Read The Basics of Preserving and Arranging, pages 10–30.

2. Follow the general directions for making potpourri, page 148. Use flowers and petals of the colors you want.

3. Pack the box tightly with yellow potpourri. Arrange pansies on top of the potpourri so the lid of the box touches the pansies.

Pack the second box tightly with blue potpourri, then make a design on top of the potpourri with one light blue delphinium in the center surrounded by darker larkspur florets.

4. Glue coordinating ribbon around the edge of each box.

5. Make two bows (see page 26) and glue to the edges of the box.

Decorated Hat Box

A decorated box filled with potpourri is made even more appealing with just a few flowers rimmed in lace. The fragrance of this box emanates from the tiny nosegay without and, when the lid is slowly lifted, from the potpourri within. (See the photograph on page 142.)

FLOWERS & FOLIAGE

Air-dried

blackberry lily (6)

lavender (22)

German statice (20)

pearly everlasting (14 dyed rose)

baby's breath (12)

Miscellaneous

sand-dried hydrangeas (10 blue)

potpourri (3 cups)

SIZE

Finished nosegay on top of box is 4½″ in diameter × 2½″ high.

MATERIALS

miniature hat box, 7″ in dia.

wrist corsage holder

floral foam 2″ long × 2″ wide × 1″ high

thick white craft glue

clear matte spray fixative

clippers

INSTRUCTIONS

1. Read The Basics of Preserving and Arranging, pages 10–30.

2. Follow the general directions for making potpourri, page 148.

3. Fill the box with approximately 3 cups of potpourri and cover with the lid.

4. Cut away the elastic bands and glue the wrist corsage holder to the boxlid. Glue the square of floral foam to the center of the holder as shown in Figure 30 on page 86.

5. Use lavender and blackberry lily stems as guidelines. Fill in with German statice, rose pearly everlasting, hydrangeas, balancing the colors and shapes of the flowers. Glue baby's breath here and there. Keep the nosegay in proportion to the size of the box lid.

6. Cover the box to protect it and spray with clear matte fixative (see page 19).

Tender Touches

The gifts that follow are easy to make, fun to give, and wonderful to receive.

From the Heart

A heart-shaped ceramic dish is filled with potpourri made of red petals and berries, topped by a red rose. In this diet-conscious age it serves as a substitute for candy and is truly a feast for the eyes. (See the photograph on page 142.)

Traditional Lavender

Lavender blossoms are a welcome addition to potpourri because of their pleasant, long-lasting fragrance. They also make delightful small gifts when sprigs are made into bunches and tied with pretty blue ribbons. (See the photograph on page 142.)

Petal Perfect

Pink peony and rose petals, along with a few miniature roses, call attention to the painted flowers on an antique Bavarian plate. (See the photograph on page 143.)

Lovely Lilies

A small bunch of lilies of the valley is a charming addition to a table, and can be tied with a ribbon of any color to match the room's color scheme. Dried lilies of the valley have what I call a "psychological scent"—their fragrance is so well known that the very sight of them evokes an imaginary aroma. (See the photograph on page 143.)

Clockwise, beginning bottom center: Peekaboo Petals; Lacy Lingerie
Fragrancers; Moss and Potpourri Basket; Cup, Saucer, and Flowers;
Decorated Hat Box; From the Heart. Center: Traditional Lavender.

Clockwise, beginning bottom left: Fanciful Fan; Finishing Flourish; Overflowing Basket; Potpourri Heart Box; Petal Perfect. Center: Lovely Lilies.

Potpourri Heart Box

A heart-shaped box is enchanting alone, but when dressed in rosy colors with the promise of a fragrant bonus inside, it is spirit-lifting as well. (See the photograph on page 143.)

FLOWERS & FOLIAGE

air-dried globe amaranth (3 pink)

sand-dried larkspur (4 pink)

silica-gel-dried miniature roses (3 pink)

pressed rose leaves (5)

potpourri (1 cup, mostly pink)

SIZE

Finished box is 5″ at the widest part × 2½″ high.

MATERIALS

decorated chipboard heart-shaped box, 5″ at the widest part

1 yd. pink ribbon ¼″ wide

thick white craft glue

clear matte spray fixative

scissors

INSTRUCTIONS

1. Read The Basics of Preserving and Arranging, pages 10–30.

2. Follow the general directions for making potpourri, page 148.

3. Fill the box with potpourri made up mostly of pink flowers and top with the lid.

4. Glue the leaves to the lid, then the other flowers as shown in the photograph. Start with the globe amaranth and larkspur, then add the roses.

5. Make a ribbon bow (see page 26) and glue it in place.

6. Cover the box to protect it and spray with clear matte fixative (see page 19).

Overflowing Basket

This basket has the look of an overflowing garden bordering a pool of potpourri. Its lush abundance speaks of summer and her bounty. (See the photograph on page 143.)

FLOWERS & FOLIAGE

Air-dried

yarrow (1 yellow, broken up)

strawflowers (6 yellow, 6 white)

statice (10 purple pieces)

salvia (16 blue)

lavender (16)

larkspur (12 pink)

cockscomb (16 pink pieces)

globe amaranth (10 pink, 10 white, 10 orange)

artemisia, stems (16)

nigella pods (4)

Miscellaneous

green sheet moss (1 yd. long × 4" wide)

Oasis Moss Mate (1 yd. long × 1" wide)

potpourri (3 cups)

SIZE

Finished basket is 9" in diameter.

MATERIALS

natural basket, 9" in diameter

thick white craft glue

clear matte spray fixative

scissors

plastic knife for glue

hot-glue gun and glue sticks (optional)

INSTRUCTIONS

1. Read The Basics of Preserving and Arranging, pages 10–30.

2. Follow the general directions for making potpourri, page 148.

3. Glue 4-inch-wide green sheet moss over the rim of the basket, 2 inches inside and 2 inches outside, to serve as a base for the floral border. Use either hot glue or craft glue for attaching mosses.

4. With strips of Moss Mate 1 inch wide, wrap the handle and glue at each end. Make the Moss Mate bow separately, wrapping the tie around the bow instead of tying it, and glue it in place.

5. Following the photograph, attach flowers to the moss around the edge of the basket with craft glue. Try to distribute the flowers evenly along all four sides, balancing the colors and shapes.

6. Spray the flowers with clear matte fixative (see page 19).

7. Fill the basket with potpourri and place whole flowers on top.

Fanciful Fan

Decorating a pretty fan with dried flowers makes it prettier still—an appropriate gift for Mother's Day. (See the photograph on page 143.)

FLOWERS & FOLIAGE 🌿

Air-dried
larkspur (3 pink)

larkspur, individual blossoms (6 pink)

pearly everlasting (4 white)

rose (1 red)

baby's breath (5)

Miscellaneous
pressed ferns (3 sprayed green)

Fig. 38. Ferns glued to fan before adding flowers

SIZE
Finished fan is 12″ long × 6″ wide.

MATERIALS
cardboard fan

3 yds. pink ribbon ¼″ wide

floral tape

thick white craft glue

clear matte spray fixative

scissors

hot-glue gun and glue sticks (optional)

INSTRUCTIONS
1. Read The Basics of Preserving and Arranging, pages 10–30.

2. Glue the ferns to the fan as shown in the Figure 38.

3. Following the photograph, glue pink larkspur stems into place over the ferns, then the larkspur blossoms and pearly everlasting. Place the red rose. Dip baby's breath into craft glue and add it to the bouquet. The flowers are put together like a one-sided vase arrangement.

4. Wrap the handle and stems with floral tape. Then, with the tape holding the ribbon in place, cover with satin ribbon.

5. Make a bow (see page 26) and glue it into place.

6. Cover the fan to protect it and spray the flowers with clear matte fixative (see page 19).

Finishing Flourish

The colors in the dried flowers decorating the gift boxes echo those in the Florentine-style wrapping paper. Any gift is enhanced by its wrappings, and only a few dried flowers are needed to set your gifts apart. Below are listed the materials used for the three packages shown in the photograph on page 143. Select colors, flowers, and quantities to complement your wrapping paper and the size of your package.

FLOWERS & FOLIAGE

Air-dried

globe amaranth (3 orange)

pearly everlasting (1 dyed peach)

strawflower (1 rust)

nigella pods (3)

baby's breath (3)

Miscellaneous

pressed leaves (3)

MATERIALS

wrapped boxes

raffia, 2 long strips

thick white craft glue

scissors

INSTRUCTIONS

1. Read The Basics of Preserving and Arranging, pages 10–30.

2. For this particular paper and color scheme, raffia seemed appropriate as a substitute for the more commonly used ribbon. Wrap the raffia around the box lengthwise and widthwise and tie a bow.

3. Glue the flowers around the bow in an attractive arrangement.

Recipe for Potpourri

Inevitably some flowers (especially if they are beyond their prime or too open) will break or fall apart in the course of picking, preserving, or arranging. That is too bad, but all is not lost. Save the flowers for potpourri. And when you've tired of an arrangement or it looks a little sad, break the flowers up for potpourri. Save the petals in separate boxes by color in case you want particular colors or layers of colors for a see-through container or a special bowl. Colors can always be mixed later but are very difficult to separate.

Potpourri, a mixture of dried flowers (or herbs, spices, roots, bark, etc.), oil, and fixative, is both fragrant and beautiful. Potpourri has been treasured since antiquity and has remained enormously popular to this day, despite the vast assortment of air deodorants and room "fresheners" that are available. Ingredients can be mixed into infinite combinations of fragrance, color, and texture. The ways of displaying or packaging potpourri are limited only by your imagination: as a lacy sachet, in a covered glass jar or box, in a seashell. (Uncovered potpourri will gradually lose its scent.)

The method of drying flowers specifically for potpourri is the same as drying flowers in general, except that you can cut the stems very short and can remove the petals before drying (although whole flowers add both beauty and texture). Material must be completely dry before being used in potpourri because moisture can cause mold. Petals shrink while drying, so prepare plenty.

A fixative is used in making potpourri to preserve and extend the fragrance. Orris root, a common fixative, is often difficult to find, and many people are allergic to it. An easy-to-find, inexpensive substitute is ground-up corncobs, called corncob bedding, for sale in pet shops. Buy the smallest pellets available, generally about ¼ inch square. Concentrated essential oil is added to enhance the scent of the flowers. Essential oils in many different fragrances are available in craft, gift, and flower shops and even in some supermarkets.

What follows is a general "recipe" for potpourri. Do experiment and create your own favorite combinations.

QUANTITY

These materials make about 9 cups of potpourri.

MATERIALS

1 cup processed corncobs (called corncob bedding)

8 cups dried flower petals and flowers

1 ounce essential oil, any fragrance

plastic bag or jar

INSTRUCTIONS

1. Mix tiny corncob pieces thoroughly with 1 ounce of essential oil in the fragrance of your choice and place in the plastic bag or jar for 24 hours.

2. Add the fragrant fixative (corncob and oil) to the petals and flowers. Keep the bag or jar closed for a day or so to allow the fragrance to mix with the petals. If the petals are very flat you may want to add more, which will weaken the perfume.

3. Display or package as you choose.

SPECIAL EFFECTS

For sheer fun with flowers, turn them into whimsical forms to suit your fancy. Dried flowers give us the freedom to try unique ideas that would not work with flowers requiring water.

Here is a melange of out-of-the-ordinary flower arrangements to delight and inspire, including an idea whose time has come—again: topiaries. A topiary is a crown of flowers topping a strong supporting potted stem. The flowers can be in the shape of a ball, a block, or a cone, depending on the designer's wishes. Every few years these charming trees are rediscovered, but with a new twist. The current pet of the floral world is constructed on a stem or stems of grapevine or other woody material, not with the stiff dowels of yesterday. To complement the natural look, dried flowers instead of artificial ones are the main attraction of the tree.

In addition, we offer suspended flowers, reflections in a flower-wreathed mirror, and a pair of darling bears.

Tops in Topiary

Here is an outstanding example of to-piary. This interpretation contains a variety of colors and flowers, with euca-lyptus giving the decoration unity. A tree like this would add beauty to a hall table or desk.

FLOWERS & FOLIAGE

Air-dried

German statice (40)

strawflowers (14 pink)

cockscomb (8 deep pink)

everlasting (20 yellow pieces)

hydrangeas (3 green, broken up)

Miscellaneous

silica-gel-dried roses (16 off-white, 12 dark red, 16 red, 3 pink)

glycerinized eucalyptus (26)

Spanish moss

SIZE

Finished topiary is 18″ high.

MATERIALS

plaster of Paris

water

plastic foam cup or similar container, 3″ in diameter × 3½″ high

woody stem for trunk ⅓ block Sahara floral foam

nylon filament (fishing line)

container for finished arrangement, 6″ in diameter × 6″ high

papier-mâchê

20″ square quilted fabric

1 yd. satin ribbon for container ½″ wide

2 yds. satin ribbon ½″ wide for tree

fine spool wire

clear matte spray fixative

measuring cup and spoon

hot-glue gun and glue sticks

knife

wire cutters

fabric stiffener or wallpaper paste

pan for mixing

INSTRUCTIONS

1. Read The Basics of Preserving and Arranging, pages 10–30.

2. Make the topiary base according to the directions on pages 23–24.

3. The container is papier-mâché covered with a piece of quilt dipped into wallpaper paste or a stiffening agent (found in craft shops). A rubber band holds the fabric in place while it dries

around the container. After the fabric is dry, decorate it with ribbon. Choose the cloth to complement the decorative style of the room.

4. Place the topiary base inside the covered container and pad under or around it as necessary. Cover the mechanics with Spanish moss.

5. Following the photograph, place the eucalyptus first, then the German statice. Be sure to turn the arrangement around while working on it to keep the topiary symmetrical. After the filler material, add color accents with the smaller flowers. Insert the strawflowers and larger blooms, then the silica-gel-dried roses.

Medley of Topiaries

These topiaries are ideal for luncheon centerpieces placed on tables decorated similarly but in different colors, giving the room a coordinated and exciting look. The inexpensive containers covered in equally inexpensive paper ribbon belie their rich look and help to keep down the cost for club luncheon decorations. The enchanting trees will be sold quickly either outright or in a fund-raising raffle.

FLOWERS & FOLIAGE
Blue Topiary

Air-dried

German statice (26 natural)

strawflowers (22 white)

salvia (30 blue)

baby's breath (15)

Sand-dried

delphinium, individual blossoms (22 light blue)

larkspur (26 blue)

yarrow (20 white, broken up)

Miscellaneous

Spanish moss

Pink Topiary

Air-dried

German statice (36 natural, 36 sprayed pink)

strawflowers (30 pink)

globe amaranth (30 pink)

cockscomb (8 pink)

baby's breath (28)

Miscellaneous

sand-dried miniature roses (8 pink)

Spanish moss

Yellow Topiary

Air-dried

German statice (36 natural)

bloom broom (36 dyed yellow)

curry plant (20 yellow pieces)

yarrow (15 yellow, broken up)

strawflowers (20 yellow)

Craspedia globosa (12 yellow)

baby's breath (10)

Miscellaneous

Spanish moss

SIZE

Finished topiary is 17" high.

MATERIALS

plaster of Paris

water

3 plastic foam cups or similar containers, 3" in diameter × 3½" high

3 woody stems for trunk

1 block Sahara floral foam

nylon filament (fishing line)

3 containers for finished arrangements, e.g., papier-mâché 5″ in diameter × 4″ high

2 yds. each blue, pink, yellow paper ribbon 4″ wide

2 yds. each blue, pink, yellow satin ribbon ½″ wide

fine spool wire

clear matte spray fixative

measuring cup and spoon

hot-glue gun and glue sticks

knife

wire cutters

INSTRUCTIONS

1. Read The Basics of Preserving and Arranging, pages 10–30.

2. Make three topiary bases according to the directions on pages 23–24.

3. Cover the papier-mâché containers with paper ribbon (see page 25). For these containers cut strips of ribbon about 16 inches long. Then cut strips of paper ribbon 1 inch wide as trim glued under the rim, and for bows (see page 25). The streamers are looped, then held in place with hot glue.

4. Place the topiary base into the decorated container. Add stuffing (newspaper, plastic bags, etc.) under and around the cup as necessary to steady it. Cover the top of the container with Spanish moss to cover the mechanics.

5. It is always important to keep turning any arrangement around while you are working on it to keep it symmetrical, but it is especially important in a topiary. Following the photographs, start by inserting the filler material, such as German statice, then add accents with smaller flowers. Place the strawflowers or slightly larger blooms, then any delicate sand-dried flowers. Glue baby's breath here and there to finish.

6. Make satin ribbon bows with streamers (see page 26) and place them at the bases of the tops with fine wire.

7. Spray with clear matte fixative (see page 19).

Mirror Wreathed in Flowers

An inexpensive mirror is magically transformed by a wreath of flowers. A delicate collection of summer's treasures are attached to a straw wreath coaxed into an oval shape to frame the mirror.

An undertaking such as this requires time, but when working with dried flowers it is not necessary to finish the project at one sitting. The time spent making this frame is well worth it since the result is not only beautiful but long-lasting.

FLOWERS & FOLIAGE

Air-dried

hydrangeas (9 green, broken up)

globe amaranth (24 white, 24 pink, 24 orange)

statice (20 white, 10 purple, 10 blue)

German statice (1 bunch)

strawflowers (12 white, 12 peach, 12 yellow, 12 pink)

curry plants (24 yellow small bunches)

pearly everlasting (small bunches: 24 white, 24 dyed rose, 24 dyed peach)

cockscomb (12 red, 12 pink)

yarrow (12 yellow)

larkspur (20 pink)

nigella pods (16)

cluster-flowered everlasting (12 yellow)

sea lavender (35)

baby's breath (35)

Sand-dried

hydrangeas (8 blue, broken up)

yarrow (4 white, broken up)

Miscellaneous

silica-gel-dried roses (10 off-white)

glycerinized goldenrod, short stems (32 dyed red)

SIZE

Finished mirror with wreath is 17" wide × 26" high.

MATERIALS

oval mirror, 15" wide × 24" high

straw wreath approximately 22" in diameter

pole pins, 1" long

strapping tape

thick white craft glue

clear matte spray fixative

scissors

clippers

INSTRUCTIONS

1. Read The Basics of Preserving and Arranging, pages 10–30. Remove the plastic wrapping from the wreath. If the wreath is fresh and pliable it can be bent into an oval shape. If it is stiff, dampen it and tie it into the desired shape and allow it to dry overnight.

2. Attach strapping tape on the inside of the wreath, then bring it over the top of the wreath, across the back of the mirror, and up around the

other side of the wreath. Bring tape as far under the second side of the wreath, close to the mirror, as possible. Repeat for the height. Shake the framed mirror to see that it holds together. If not, add more tape next to the first. See Figure 39 for taping.

3. Most mirrors of this type have a hook on the back, but if yours does not, add a wire hanger to the wreath as described on page 22 before attaching the wreath to the mirror.

4. Using Figure 16 on page 28 as a guide, turn branched flowers such as goldenrod and German statice into small bunches before attaching them to the wreath.

5. Start on the outside of the wreath and work in rows horizontally across toward the mirror, attaching flowers to the straw with pole pins as shown in Figure 31 on page 106. Glue flowers where pins won't fit. The top of the second row of flowers should just cover the pins of the previous row; do not place one bunch on top of an-

other or the wreath will be too bulky. If you prefer, you can use glue to attach all the flowers. Check to see that flowers, not straw, are reflected at the edge of the mirror.

There is no particular order in which you should fill the wreath, but you do want to distribute the flowers evenly all around. You might start by placing pieces of green hydrangea all around the wreath. Following the photograph, keep the flowers, colors, and shapes well balanced. As you work, check often to make sure you have enough of any flower left to go all around the wreath. Use the air-dried flowers first, then the sand-dried, and finally the silica-gel-dried roses. Finish decorating by gluing the airy stems of baby's breath and sea lavender here and there.

6. Cover the mirror to protect it and spray the wreath with at least two light coats of clear matte spray fixative (see page 19).

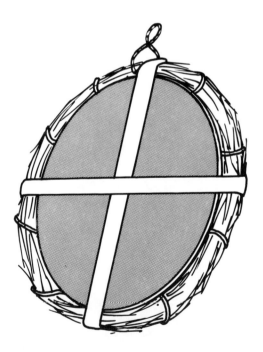

Fig. 39. Taping straw wreath to mirror

Floral Bears

These whimsical flower-coated bears are long-lasting decorations that are also perfect welcome-home gifts for a new mother. It is not necessary to complete a bear in one sitting.

FLOWERS & FOLIAGE

Air-dried

globe amaranth (1,200 white)

yarrow (10 yellow, broken up)

Miscellaneous

sand-dried black-eyed Susans (3)

Fig. 40. Foam base for Mother Bear

Mother Bear

The mother bear's base is floral foam for dried flowers, and her coat of white globe amaranth is held in place with craft glue.

SIZE

Finished larger bear is 10½ " wide × 14" high.

MATERIALS

3 blocks floral foam

thick white craft glue

dowel ½ " in diameter, approximately 24" long

½ yd. green velveteen ribbon ¾" wide

clear matte spray fixative

knife

plastic knife for glue

INSTRUCTIONS

1. Read The Basics of Preserving and Arranging, pages 10–30.

2. To make the form for the bear, shown in Figure 40, stand one block of floral foam vertically for the body and cut the second block in half. Use a piece 4 inches × 4 inches × 3 inches for the head. Dip each end of a 2-inch piece of dowel in glue, then push one end into the head and the other into the body to hold them together. Cut the other half in half for the legs, each measuring 2 inches wide × 3 inches high. Cut a notch in the leg where it meets the body so it will fit closely, as shown in the illustration, and attach to the body with dowels 2 inches long.

Cut the arms 3½ inches × 2 inches × 2 inches, notch, and attach to the body with 2-inch dowels. Cut the ears in a circle 2½ inches in diameter

by ½ inch thick, notch, and attach to the head with shorter dowels. Cut a piece for the stomach 2½ inches wide × 4 inches high × 1½ inches deep, trim it into a curve, and attach it to the body with a 2-inch dowel. Cut foam 2 inches wide × 4 inches high × 1½ inches deep, trim into a curve for the nose, and attach with a dowel. Use leftover pieces to pad the side of the body by 1½ inches and the head by 1 inch. Hold padding in place with 2-inch dowels.

3. Allow glue holding dowels to set overnight.

4. Starting from the bottom and working up, as you would when frosting a cake, spread an inch or two of glue at least ¼ inch thick. Push the heads of globe amaranth into the glue. Then cover the next inch or two with glue, push in the globe amaranth, and repeat.

5. Break up the yarrow into small stems before gluing it to the paws and the ears as shown in the photograph.

6. The nose and the flowers to be used for eyes should be added after the head is covered with its floral coat. The nose is the center of a black-eyed Susan, with the wire still attached. To attach the features use the wires they dried on, or add fine spool wire.

7. Make a ribbon bow, glue it in place, and allow the bear at least one day to dry before moving it.

8. Spray with at least two light coats of clear matte fixative (see page 19).

Baby Bear

This fuzzy-looking floral baby bear is pure joy. Like his mother he is time-consuming to create. But he can be covered a little at a time and is certain to delight.

FLOWERS & FOLIAGE

air-dried yarrow (25 yellow, broken up)
sand-dried black-eyed Susans (3 centers)

SIZE

Finished smaller bear is 8″ wide × 7½″ high.

MATERIALS

1 block floral foam
dowel ¼″ in diameter, approximately 24″
thick white craft glue
½ yd. green velveteen ribbon ⅝″ wide
clear matte spray fixative
knife
plastic knife for glue

INSTRUCTIONS

1. Read The Basics of Preserving and Arranging, pages 10–30.

2. Cut foam in quarters widthwise. Use one quarter, measuring 4 inches × 2 inches × 2 inches, for the body. Cut the next quarter in half for the head, which will measure 2 inches × 2 inches × 3 inches. Attach the head to the body with a short piece of dowel that has been dipped in glue at each end. (See Figure 41.)

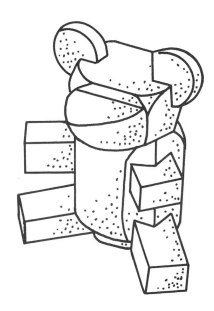

Fig. 41. Foam base for Baby Bear

The third quarter is cut into fourths lengthwise, two pieces for the legs and two pieces for the arms. Cut 1½ inches off the ends of the legs, notch one end of each leg, and attach to the body with dowel sections. Cut 2 inches off the ends of the arms to make them measure 2 inches × 1 inch × 1 inch, notch, and attach to body as shown in the illustration.

The ears are 1½ inches × 1½ inches × ½ inch, notched, and attached to head with dowels. The stomach protrudes from the body 1½ inches and is 1½ inches wide × 3 inches high. The nose, cut 2½ inches wide × 1½ inches high, protrudes 1 inch from the head. The head and body can be padded with leftover scraps attached with dowels.

3. Allow the dowel glue to dry overnight before attaching flowers.

4. Proceed with gluing as for the Mother Bear. Break yarrow into smaller stems before pushing into the glue. Apply one or two inches of glue, at least ¼ inch thick, to the bottom of the bear. Continue gluing upwards an inch or two at a time.

5. The eyes and nose are the centers of black-eyed Susans. Attach them with the wires they dried on, or add fine spool wire.

6. Make a ribbon bow, glue it in place, and allow the bear to dry before moving it.

7. Spray with two light coats of clear matte fixative (see page 19).

Flowers in Space

This hanging bouquet would be at home in a window, a dark corner, anywhere it would lend a cheery note. Normally dried flowers should not be placed in direct light, but because this bouquet is made of plants that are sturdy and not particularly colorful, they will keep their ethereal look even if they fade.

FLOWERS & FOLIAGE

Air-dried

pearly everlasting (32 white, 32 pink, 32 dyed peach)

nigella pods (32)

salvia (22 blue)

globe amaranth (20 pink)

eucalyptus (14)

statice (10 purple)

larkspur (14 blue)

rhodanthe (10 pink, 10 white)

artemisia, stems (42)

heather (20)

goldenrod, heads (4 red, 4 yellow)

Miscellaneous

raffia (3 long pieces)

SIZE

Finished arrangement is approximately 15" in diameter.

MATERIALS

2 plastic berry boxes, 3½" square × 2½" high

½ block floral foam

fine spool wire

clear matte spray fixative

scissors

knife

clippers

INSTRUCTIONS

1. Read The Basics of Preserving and Arranging, pages 10–30.

2. Cut floral foam to fit into one berry box, then cut four corners of the other box and force it over the first. Tie it with fine wire as shown in Figure 42. Make a wire loop at the top to receive the raffia.

Fig. 42. Berry-box base for Flowers in Space

3. Tie three pieces of raffia to the loop to serve as a hanger, then hang the box temporarily at eye level for easy arranging.

4. Insert short stems (about 3 inches long) of the larger flowers into the openings in the berry boxes. Good choices are nigella pods, blue salvia, pink globe amaranth, blue larkspur, and pink and white rhodanthe. When the boxes are

completely covered add the longer-stemmed flowers such as eucalyptus, white and peach pearly everlasting, and artemisia to give the arrangement a light and airy look. These stems should vary between 4 and 6 inches in length.

5. Spray with clear matte fixative (see page 19).

6. Attach a bow and streamers of raffia, adding to the arrangement's ethereal look.

APPENDIX

SOURCES FOR SUPPLIES

For floral supplies and equipment, check your local florists, nurseries, craft and hobby shops.

To order by mail, send a self-addressed stamped envelope (SASE) for a price list.

FLORAL SUPPLIES

Dorothy Biddle Service
Greeley, PA. 18425-9799

Lamartine Square Floral Supplies
Box 504, Mt. Vernon, Ohio 43050

DRIED FLOWERS

Good Scents
P.O. Box 854
Rialto, CA. 92377
Tel.: 714-876-5783
Catalog is 50 cents

Backyard Herbs 'n Things
4101 Canfield Rd.
Canfield, OH 44406
Tel.: 216-793-8326
Catalog available

Countree
4573 Bender Rd.
Middleville, MI 49333
Tel.: 616-795-7132
Price list available

The Peaceable Kingdom
8375 Rapid Lightning Rd.
Sandpoint, ID 83864
Tel.: 208-263-8038
Catalog available for 45-cent stamp

The Rosemary House, Inc.
120 South Market St.
Mechanicsburg, PA 17055
Tel.: 717-766-6581
Catalog available for $2.00

Tom Thumb Workshops
Rt. 13, P.O. Box 357
Mappsville, VA 23407
Tel.: 804-824-3507
Catalog available for $1.00

ESSENTIAL OILS

Mrs. O'Quinn's Scent Shoppe
1908 Joann St.
Wichita, KS 67203
Tel.: 316-264-6344
Price list available

DRIED FLOWERS BY COLOR

WHITE, OFF-WHITE, AND SILVER

Artemisia
Baby's breath
Caspia
Delphinium
Dogwood
Echinops
Eucalyptus
Feverfew
Globe amaranth
Hyacinth blossom
Lamb's ear
Larkspur
Lily of the valley
Nigella
Pearly everlasting
Peony
Pussy willow
Queen Anne's lace
Ranunculus
Rose
Statice sinuata
Strawflower
White yarrow
Zinnia

GREEN

Dock
Hydrangea
Grasses
Ferns
Mint

BROWN

Dock
Glycerinized leaves
Sweet Annie (artemisia)
Teasel

YELLOW

Black-eyed Susan
Craspedia
Cluster flowered everlasting
Curry plant
Daffodil
Goldenrod
Marigold
Pansy
Snapdragon
Statice sinuata
Strawflower
Zinnia

ORANGE

Globe amaranth
Marigold
Strawflower

BLUE

Blue salvia
Cornflower
Delphinium
Dutch iris
Hydrangea
Larkspur
Lavender
Nigella
Statice sinuata

PURPLE

Dahlia
Globe amaranth
Pansy
Statice sinuata
Zinnia

PINK

Astilbe

Carnation
Chive blossom
Cockscomb
Dahlia
Delphinium
Globe amaranth
Heather
Larkspur
Peony
Ranunculus
Rose
Rat's tail statice
Strawflower
Tulip
Zinnia

RED

Cockscomb
Ranunculus
Rose
Salvia
Zinnia

Index

All of us at Sedgewood® Press are dedicated to offering you, our customer, the best books we can create. We are particularly concerned that all of the instructions for making the projects are clear and accurate. We welcome your comments and would like to hear any suggestions you may have. Please address your correspondence to Customer Service Department, Sedgewood® Press, Meredith Corporation, 750 Third Avenue, New York, NY 10017

For information on how you can have *Better Homes and Gardens* delivered to your door, write to: Mr. Robert Austin, P.O. Box 4536, Des Moines, IA 50336.